Borges Revisited

Twayne's World Authors Series

Latin American Literature

David W. Foster, Editor

Arizona State University

TWAS 819

Jorge Luis Borges
Photograph courtesy of Lütfi Özkök.

Borges Revisited

Martin S. Stabb

The Pennsylvania State University

Twayne Publishers • Boston
A Division of G. K. Hall & Co.

Borges Revisited
Martin S. Stabb

Copyright 1991 by G.K. Hall & Co.
All rights reserved.
Published by Twayne Publishers
A division of G.K. Hall & Co.
70 Lincoln Street
Boston, Massachusetts 02111

Copyediting supervised by Barbara Sutton.
Book production by Janet Z. Reynolds.
Book design by Barbara Anderson.
Typeset by Compositors Corp., Cedar Rapids, Iowa.

10 9 8 7 6 5 4 3 2 1

The paper used in this publication meets the minimum requirements
of American National Standard for Information Sciences—Permanence
of Paper for Printed Library Materials, ANSI Z39.48–1984. ⊚™
Printed and bound in the United States of America.

Library of Congress Cataloging-in-Publication Data

Stabb, Martin S.
    Borges revisited / Martin S. Stabb.
        p.   cm. — (Twayne's world authors series ; TWAS 819. Latin
American literature)
    Includes bibliographical references.
    ISBN 0-8057-8263-X (alk. paper)
    1. Borges, Jorge Luis, 1899-   —Criticism and interpretation.
2. Borges, Jorge Luis, 1899-   —Influence. 3. Literature,
Modern—20th century—History and criticism. I. Title.
II. Series: Twayne's world authors series ; TWAS 819. III. Series:
Twayne's world authors series. Latin American literature.
PQ7797.B635Z9178   1991
868—dc20   90-48714

For Gloria
"... como una dicha en la selección del recuerdo"

Contents

Preface

When my *Jorge Luis Borges* appeared in 1970, Borges was still a rather mysterious figure among English-speaking readers, despite the fact that much of his work had been translated and that studies analyzing his unusual narratives were beginning to circulate. Yet at the time it seemed that his literary activity was waning. With the exception of one major collection, *El hacedor (Dreamtigers),* published at the very start of the sixties, the decade saw him produce only a modest number of poems, some works in collaboration, revisions or reworkings of earlier texts, and virtually no new stories. Travel, teaching as a guest of foreign universities, a short-lived unsuccessful marriage, his increasing blindness, or other personal factors perhaps explain this dearth of literary output. Then, to the surprise of many who considered his career to be drawing to a close, the frail, seventy-year-old published an impressive collection of prose pieces, *El informe de Brodie (Doctor Brodie's Report,* 1970); a volume of poetry, *Elogio de la sombra (In Praise of Darkness,* 1969); followed shortly by a collection of prose and poetry, *El oro de los tigres (The Gold of the Tigers,* 1972); another book of stories, *El libro de arena (The Book of Sand,* 1973); several more volumes of poetry and other miscellaneous collections. In short, he continued as an active writer almost until his death in June 1986.

Many critics would hold that Borges's greatest achievements came in the early years, especially the forties and fifties, though this view could be challenged. One of the objectives of this volume is to address the question of the early or "canonical" Borges versus the later Borges. Another objective is to make a fresh assessment of the Argentine master's position as a major Western literary presence. While he had gained considerable fame beyond Latin America by the late sixties, it is only recently that highly sophisticated theorists in Europe and America have come to recognize him as a key figure in the shaping of late-twentieth-century literary—and critical—trends. An interesting peripheral question concerns Borges's relationship to the highly successful "new narrative" of Latin America, a movement that has in effect transformed the continent's image from that of a derivative, picturesque area to one characterized by tremendous creativity and impressive technical achievement.

Obviously a considerable portion of this volume is devoted to discussion and analysis of Borges's work from the late sixties until his death. As in my earlier study, the prose fiction, poetry, and essayistic writings are all examined. Although I emphasize the later writings and more recent critical perspectives, I have included sufficient material on Borges's early work and early life to provide a comprehensive view of his career. One important omission should be noted. Space does not permit any discussion of the work that Borges produced in collaboration, especially the items co-authored with his close friend Adolfo Bioy Casares. These works, however, are noted in the Bibliography.

In my citations of Borges's prose only English translations appear: this seems justified since a very large proportion of his prose work is readily available in English. In a few cases, where no English version has been published, I use my own translation. While some of Borges's better known poems have been translated, a great deal of his early poetry (and some of the later work) is only available in Spanish. Moreover, the quality of the poetic translations is, in my view, somewhat unequal. At any rate, I have chosen to use my own translations of the poetry and to include the original Spanish parenthetically in the text. Any exceptions are, of course, noted. The dates of publication for works cited in the text refer to the original Spanish editions. Included in parentheses are English versions of the titles: Roman type indicates that no translation is available whereas italics or quotation marks indicate that an English version has been published. The dates for these translations appear only in the Bibliography.

In the twenty years that have elapsed since the publication of *Jorge Luis Borges,* Latin American literature has emerged as one of the most acclaimed expressions of contemporary literary art to be found in the Western world. Recognition has come in the form of widespread translations, abundant critical acclaim in prestigious international circles, and in the awarding of several recent Nobel prizes to Spanish American writers. Despite the fact that he never wrote novels, perhaps the most popular of modern literary genres, that his mild liberalism was at odds with the prevailing socialist/Marxist radicalism of Latin America's intellectuals, and that he was not a Nobel laureate, Borges has gained a place among the most celebrated writers of the hemisphere. It also seems likely that even in the broader context of the Western literary tradition he will long be regarded as a genuine twentieth-century master. It is my hope that readers of *Borges Revisited* will gain some insight into how and why this has come about.

Chronology

1899   Jorge Luis Borges born 24 August in Buenos Aires, the son of Jorge Borges and Leonor Acevedo de Borges.

1914   Travels with his family to Europe. At outbreak of World War I, he is forced to remain in Geneva, Switzerland, where he attends secondary school.

1919   Travels in Spain, and publishes several poems under the influence of the Spanish *Ultraísta* movement.

1921   Returns to Buenos Aires. Collaborates on "billboard review" *Prisma* and edits the manifesto "Ultraísmo" published in the magazine *Nosotros*.

1922   With several others, founds the review *Proa*.

1923   Makes second trip to Europe. His first collection of verse, *Fervor de Buenos Aires* (Fervor of Buenos Aires), is published.

1924   With others, founds the second *Proa*.

1925   *Luna de enfrente* (Moon across the way) and his first essay collection, *Inquisiciones* (Inquisitions), appear.

1926   *El tamaño de mi esperanza* (The size of my hope) published.

1928   *El idioma de los argentinos* (The language of the Argentines).

1929   Publishes *Cuaderno San Martín* (San Martin notebook) and receives second prize in municipal literary contest.

1930   *Evaristo Carriego (Evaristo Carriego)*.

1932   *Discusión* (Discussion).

1935   First collection of narrative prose, *Historia universal de la infamia (A Universal History of Infamy)*, appears.

1936   *Historia de la eternidad* (A history of eternity).

1937   With Pedro Henríquez Ureña, publishes *Antología clásica de la literatura argentina* (A classical anthology of Argentine literature).

1938   After the death of his father, takes post as assistant librarian in a small municipal library. Late in year, suffers accident and is hospitalized for several weeks.

1940   With Silvina Ocampo and A. Bioy Casares, publishes *Antología de la literature fantástica* (An anthology of fantastic literature).

1941   First collection of stories, *El jardín de senderos que se bifurcan* (The garden of the forking paths), appears. With Silvina Ocampo and A. Bioy Casares, publishes *Antología poética argentina* (An anthology of Argentine poetry).

1942   The magazine *Sur* dedicates a special issue to Borges on the occasion of his not being awarded the National Prize for Literature. With A. Bioy Casares, publishes *Seis problemas para don Isidro Parodi* (*Six Problems for Don Isidro Parodi*).

1943   Under pseudonym B. Suárez Lynch, edits *Los mejores cuentos policiales* (Best detective stories).

1944   *Ficciones (Ficciones)*. Receives "Prize of Honor" from the Sociedad Argentina de Escritores.

1946   With Bioy Casares, publishes *Dos fantasías memorables* (Two memorable fantasies) and *Un modelo para la muerte* (A model for death).

1947   *Nueva refutación del tiempo* (A new refutation of time).

1949   *El Aleph (The Aleph and Other Stories)*.

1951   With Delia Ingenieros, publishes *Antiguas literaturas germánicas* (Ancient Germanic literatures); and, with Bioy Casares, the second series of *Los mejores cuentos policiales* (Best detective stories).

1952   *Otras inquisiciones (Other Inquisitions)*.

1953   With Margarita Guerrero, *El "Martín Fierro"* (The Martin Fierro).

1955   Becomes director of the National Library after fall of Perón. In collaboration with Bioy Casares, publishes *Los orilleros* (The slum-dwellers) and *El paraíso de los creyentes* (The paradise of the believers) (unproduced screenplays). Named member of the Argentine Academy of Letters.

1956   Appointed professor of English Literature at the University of Buenos Aires. Receives honorary doctorate from University of Cuyo. Awarded National Prize for Literature.

1957   With Margarita Guerrero, *Manual de zoolgía fantástica* (A manual of fantastic zoology).

1960   *El hacedor (Dreamtigers)*. With Bioy Casares, *Libro del cielo y del infierno (The Book of Imaginary Beings)*.

1961   Shares the internationally prestigious Prix Formentor with Samuel

Beckett. Publishes *Antología personal (A Personal Anthology)*. Invited to teach in United States at University of Texas. Travels and lectures in United States.

1963   Travels and lectures in England, France, Spain, and Switzerland.

1967   In September marries Elsa Astete Millán (Widow of Ricardo Albarracín Sarmiento). Is invited to teach at Harvard University as Charles Eliot Norton Lecturer.

1968   Returns to Buenos Aires.

1970   *El informe de Brodie (Doctor Brodie's Report)* and *Elogio de la sombra (In Praise of Darkness)* published. Lectures in Israel. Divorced.

1971   Awarded honorary doctorate from Columbia University and Jerusalem Prize.

1972   *El oro de los tigres (The Gold of the Tigers)*.

1973   Perón regains the presidency; Borges resigns as director of the National Library.

1975   *El libro de arena (The Book of Sand)*, *La rosa profunda* (The profound rose), and *Prólogos* (Prologues), a collection of prefaces, published. Borges's mother dies, age 99.

1976   *La moneda de hierro* (The iron coin). With Adolfo Bioy Casares, *Crónicas de Bustos Domecq (Chronicles of Bustos Domecq)*.

1977   *Historia de la noche*.

1981   *La cifra* (The cipher). Receives honorary degree from Harvard University.

1982   *Nueve ensayos dantescos* (Nine Dantesque essays). Delivers William James lecture at the New York Institute for the Humanities.

1983   *Veinticinco de agosto 1983 y otros cuentos* (The twenty-fifth of August 1983 and other stories).

1984   *Atlas (Atlas)*. Travels in Europe with María Kodama.

1985   *Los conjurados* (The plotters).

1986   Marries María Kodama. Shortly afterward, dies in Geneva of cancer of the liver, 14 June.

Chapter One

The Making of a Writer

It was once the fashion among literary critics to explain a writer's work on the basis of biographical facts, psychological speculation, and the nature of the formative environment. Since the mid-twentieth century, the predominant trend has been away from such approaches. Thus some critics, perhaps a bit too stridently, have stressed the notion that the text speaks for itself, that literary language is "self-referential" or "ontogenetic," that there is "nothing outside the text," or that writing only acquires aesthetic richness by virtue of its intertextuality, its mirroring of other literary works. It would be inappropriate here to become involved in the complex polemics suggested by these theoretical positions. However, given their force, it now seems that to speak of the extratextual "out there" of reality underlying the work of a given writer—such mundane things as what an author's birthplace was like, what the nature of his family situation was, or how the political atmosphere impinged upon literary life—has become a questionable activity, one that puts us on the defensive. This is doubly so in the case of Jorge Luis Borges because the details of his life have limited significance or interest except as they mark the trajectory of his remarkable literary career. My own view is that kept in perspective, biographical and background data are necessary first steps preceding critical analysis. It is in this spirit that a brief discussion of Borges's formative years is offered.

The Passion of Buenos Aires

On 14 June 1986, just a few months before reaching his eighty-seventh birthday, Borges died in Geneva, Switzerland. Only two years earlier, in one of his last books, a dreamlike, autumnal collection of travel memoirs titled *Atlas*, he prophetically wrote "I know that I will always return to Geneva, perhaps after the death of my body."[1] But in the same text he also reflects, "My physical body may be in Lucerne, Colorado, or Cairo, but each morning when I awake, when once again I take on the habit of being Borges, I invariably emerge from a dream which takes place in Buenos Aires. . . . I never dream in the present, but only of a past-tense Buenos Aires. . . . Does all this mean that beyond the limits of my will and consciousness I am irreparably, incomprehensibly, a *porteño,* a native-born descendant of the people of Buenos Aires?"[2] To those familiar with Borges this question comes as no surprise, despite the fact that perhaps more than any other Latin American writer he has transcended the limitations and provinciality of being "merely an Argentine," as he slyly referred to himself. Indeed the rich corpus of his work—poetry, essays, and above all fiction—is haunted by the ghosts of yesteryear's Buenos Aires.

It was in the heart of this city that Jorge Luis Borges was born on 24 August 1899. The Borgeses were a well-established, financially comfortable criollo family whose antecedents could be traced back to the wars of independence. One branch of the family—that represented by his paternal grandmother, Fanny Haslam—was English. Borges's father, a writer, jurist, and student of modern languages, apparently knew English well, as did young "Georgie"—as Jorge Luis came to be called. Borges did not attend school until he was nine; his education was entrusted to an English tutor, a Miss Tink. His father, too, played an important part in shaping his son's nascent literary interests. Borges's earliest memories go back to the family home in the Palermo district of Buenos Aires and more specifically to "a garden . . . and a library of limitless English books." It was here that Borges first whetted his literary appetite on narrations of adventure in distant lands; Robert Louis Stevenson and Kipling were among his earliest favorites. Friends of the family recall the young Borges's odd fascination with exotic beasts, especially the Indian tiger, an animal whose image and metaphor was to haunt many a page of the mature writer. An Argentine book on his work even reproduces a sketch of a tiger that "Georgie" drew (in a book of English nursery rhymes) at the age of four.[3] Borges's acquaintance with Hispanic literature came after his early exposure to English letters. This fact is not surprising in view of his family's cultivation of things English and considering the relative paucity of juvenile literature in Spanish. The first Argentine works he read as a boy were Eduardo Gutiérrez's gauchesque adventure novels—a literary genre rather like the North American "dime Westerns" of yesteryear. As a child he also tasted the more customary fare of the Hispanic tradition: classic works such as the *Quijote* and the epic of the Cid.

The warmth of Borges's boyhood recollections is obvious to any reader of his work, particularly to those who know his poetry. Family life, in typical Latin fashion, was close-knit and protective. His sister Norah was a constant companion; his relationship with his grandparents, especially with his English grandmother, was warm. Visitors came to the Borges household frequently, and many were men of considerable literary stature. Some of these family friends, men such as the poet Evaristo Carriego and the eccentric philosophic prose writer Macendonio Fernández, became personal and literary deities in the eyes of the young Borges.

Shortly before the start of World War I the Borgeses visited Europe. The war broke out while the family was in Geneva, and here they remained until 1918. During this period Borges's literary appetite appears to have been voracious; he read Hugo and Baudelaire in French, Heine and the works of the nascent expressionists in German. While in Switzerland Borges also discovered two authors who came to occupy central positions in his thought: Schopenhauer and Chesterton. With the end of the war, the Borges family continued their European travels. In 1919 they visited Barcelona and then Majorca. For some three years following, the family traveled on the Spanish mainland, residing in Seville and Madrid.

Borges's first real literary efforts are a number of poems composed during his Spanish travels. However, he considers the work of this period (1919–21) to be inferior and has permitted only a very few of these pieces to be reprinted in collections of his poetry. The Spanish writers whom Borges met and with whom he collaborated were a colorful group of experimental poets, the so-called *ultraístas* (ultraists) Guillermo de Torre, Rafael Cansinos Assens, and their followers. Viewed as a European literary movement, *ultraísmo* shared much of the spirit of the contemporaneous Dada, surrealism, and perhaps expressionism. From the strictly Hispanic viewpoint, it was a prolongation of the reaction against nineteenth-century poetic values, that an earlier group, the poets of 1898, had initiated. The influence of *ultraísmo* on Borges will be noted later; of greater interest at this point is Cansinos Assens's description of his twenty-year-old Argentine friend: "smiling, full of discreet serenity, urbane, even-tempered, with a poet's ardor held in check by a fortunate intellectual coldness; having a classical culture of Greek philosophy and Oriental troubadours making him fond of the past . . . of Latin dictionaries and folio manuscripts, but without making him deprecate modern wonders . . ."[4]

The family returned to Buenos Aires in 1921, an event that unquestionably moved Borges deeply. Despite his fondness for Europe and for the culture of the Old World, Borges's feelings toward his country and especially toward his native city were always characterized by a profound and almost filial love. His poem, "Arrabal" ("Neighborhood"), written the year of his return, gives some indication of these sentiments: "The years that I have spent in Europe are illusory, / I have always been (and shall always be) in Buenos Aires" ("los años que he vivido en Europa son ilusorios, / yo he estado siempre [y estaré] en Buenos Aires").[5] I have already noted how the same feelings persisted into his twilight years.

The Argentina the Borges family found upon their return differed from the country they had left. By 1914 Buenos Aires had passed the 1,500,000 mark: though the war had temporarily halted the stream of immigration that had been flowing toward the Río de la Plata, with the end of the conflict the city resumed its phenomenal growth. The economy, despite the brief postwar slump, was changing and expanding. New industries— mining and petroleum exploitation—were developed during the period of wartime isolation and provided the basis for an accelerated program of modernization. Despite the new subway, the glare of electric lights, and the gleaming modern construction, the individuality of many of the old neighborhoods (the *barrios*) was, at least for a time, preserved. Like small towns within the metropolis, Palermo, Belgrano, or Avellaneda had their own tree-lined streets, quiet patios, bars, dance halls, intimate cliques, and local gossip. In a sense, *barrio* life was a prolongation of nineteenth-century Argentina into the more dynamic, higher-pressured world of the twentieth. As such, it held great charm for the young Borges, who after an absence of seven years no doubt felt out of step with a Buenos Aires that no longer conformed to the pattern of his childhood memories. The lovely poems of his first collection, centered as they are on the patio, the older sections of the city, the quiet retreat of parks and cemeteries, are clearly products of his desire to capture the essence of a world that was fast disappearing.

By the early 1920s Borges's career had commenced in earnest. Together with a group of young writers rather like his Spanish circle, he undertook the publication of a literary review, the writing of poetic manifestos, and, most important, the polishing of a distinctive poetic style. His first venture, the review *Prisma,* is indicative of his group's mood and orientation. A "magazine" of art and poetry, *Prisma* was not circulated in the usual manner; instead it was prepared on large sign paper and then plastered on walls and fences. It was a gift to the people of Buenos Aires. As one of Borges's collaborators proclaimed, "We have bedecked the streets with poetry, we have illumined your path with verbal lamps, we have girded your walls with vines of verse!"[6] There is a certain joie de vivre in this gesture, a certain youthful playfulness that Borges retained over the years. For the Argentine *ultraístas* of the early 1920s, literature was a game, a pleasant and rather aristocratic sport for bright young sophisticates. The formal tenets of the movement (emphasis on metaphor, free rather than rhymed verse, and the elimination of superfluous poetic adornments) are made clear in the "Ultraist Manifesto," edited by Borges and published in the magazine

Nosotros, a bastion of the literary establishment.[7] As a well-defined movement, *ultraísmo* was shortlived, though its spirit lingered on. Argentine writers who held to a position of social commitment in literature were, and continue to be, cool toward the group; for unlike some of the European movements of the vanguard, the *ultraístas* were—as writers—politically aloof, ambivalent in their assessment of human progress, and decidedly not Marxist. Though he may have shared some of these general attitudes, Borges repudiated the formal tenets of *ultraísmo* almost as soon as he began publishing his poetry.

The mid-1920s was an active period for Borges. Three major collections of poetry were published in 1923, 1925, and 1929, respectively, while his first collection of essays, *Inquisiciones* (Inquisitions), appeared in 1925, followed by *El tamaño de mi esperanza* (The size of my hope) in 1926. Following the ephemeral "mural-review" *Prisma,* Borges joined forces with a somewhat different group in order to publish another literary magazine. *Proa.* More significant than the journal itself was Borges's association with several new writers, the most influential of whom was the eccentric humorist-philosopher Macedonio Fernández. To fully appreciate this relationship it is necessary to read the edition of Fernández's work that Borges lovingly prepared years later (1961). Significantly, one of the things he singles out in discussing his friend's work is the fact that "those who are called intellectuals today are not really so, since they make of their intelligence a job, or an instrument for action."[8] But, Borges notes, "Macedonio was a pure thinker. . . . He possessed to a high degree the arts of inaction and solitude."[9] Borges accepted other aspects of Macedonio Fernández's curious view of the world and of intellectuals, as we shall note later.

One of the most interesting periods in Borges's literary life began in 1924 when, on his return from a second trip to Europe, he began writing for the satirical avant-garde review *Martín Fierro.* His association with the *Martinfierrista* group is significant. This group believed in art for art's sake, in literature as "diversion" rather than as an instrument for social criticism and amelioration. Another clique of writers, chiefly those who gathered about certain leftist journals, formed the opposition and espoused what would today be called a literature of commitment. Curiously, the two bands, the more effete literary aristocrats of the *Martín Fierro* (known also as the *Florida* group) and the so-called *Boedo* group on the left, knew each other well and were often close friends. Those familiar with the Buenos Aires literary scene of the mid-1920s have even suggested that this "division" of the city's young writers into opposing camps was little more than a deliberate and consequently superficial imitation of European literary fac-

tionalism, if not a mere joke. Borges made no direct contribution to the literary polemics that engaged the two groups, yet his compatriots are loath to
forget that he was a *Martinfierrista*. They have always assumed that his
writing should reflect the playful, aristocratic, and "disengaged" attitudes of
this group. Whether or not such an assessment of Borges is valid is a question that can only be answered after his multiform work is examined.

Borges became famous as a writer through his prose rather than through
his poetry. Today he is usually thought of first as the creator of fictional labyrinths, then as the writer of erudite short essays, often on arcane subjects,
and only last as a poet. Yet he began as a poet and has worked more or less
continuously in this genre. Most important, he reveals more of himself in his
verse than in any other kind of writing. The capriciousness and learned fri-
volity of much of his prose are rarely found in his poetry. By contrast, we see
in it the other Borges—the sincere and ardent youth of the twenties or the
contemplative and nostalgic writer of the sixties and seventies. For many
this is an unknown Borges; perhaps it is the real Borges.

Borges's career as a poet and writer began when he was in his late teens.
His travels in Europe and contact with the Spanish avant-garde has already been noted. Like most young literary rebels, the members of the
circle with whom he first became associated, the *ultraístas*, craved innovation and were repelled by the tastes of their fathers. The poetic movement
against which they were reacting was *modernismo*, a rich and complex style
of writing that drew heavily on the French fin de siècle poets: Valéry,
Rimbaud, Leconte de Lisle, and others. Led by the Nicaraguan Rubén
Darío, and in Argentina by Leopoldo Lugones, *modernismo* dominated
Hispanic letters—in Spain as well as the New World—through the 1890s
and well into the twentieth century. It would be impossible to characterize
the movement adequately here. It is sufficient to say that on the formal
level, the *modernistas* endeavored to revitalize the poetic lexicon by replac-
ing the tired adjectives of romanticism with new and unusual ones; they
experimented with long-forgotten metrical schemes as well as with innovative ones; and perhaps most interestingly, they sought to blend, confuse,
and interchange the distinct sensory realms in their poetry. Following the
French poets Baudelaire and Rimbaud, they attempted to establish "cor-
respondences" between sound and color. Taking what the Parnassians had
done in their poetry as a point of departure, they tried to create verbal stat-
uary in which the precise tactile and visual terms replaced the romantic's
overt egocentrism and emotive vocabulary. From Verlaine they acquired
the notion that words possess an inherent musical quality which might be
the very essence of poetry. The content of *modernista* poetry, like its form,

differed substantially from the literature that preceded it. The newer poets preferred the artificial, whereas the romantics glorified the world of nature. They held to theories of detachment and objectivity, whereas the romantics exalted the ego and cultivated literary confessionalism. The poets of the 1890s shunned overt political or social involvement, whereas many of their predecessors had been activists and reformers. The *modernistas,* like the romantics, enjoyed decorating their poetry with the trappings of a distant age, but when they sought escape into the past their favorite periods were the Renaissance and the classical age in contrast to the romantic's love of the medieval. Finally, the typical *modernista* tried hard to avoid the romantic's penchant for the picturesque: hence he did not concern himself with the Indian, the *fatherland,* or local color. Instead he wrote of the court of Versailles or of the sensuous refinement of ancient Greece. Though the Spanish American *modernistas* imitated their European mentors to a great extent, their poetry—particularly the best pieces of the leading writers—had much originality.

It would be inaccurate to claim that Borges's poetry, even that of the early *ultraísta* period, was merely a reaction to *modernismo.* It is true that he wished to purge his poetry of certain specific *modernista* techniques and mannerisms, but like all good poets his objective was to affirm his own poetic values rather than to refute those of his predecessors. Borges admits that he never adhered to the position sketched out in his "Ultraist Manifesto" of 1921. The points he emphasized are nonetheless worth enumerating: the reduction of lyricism to metaphor; the combining of several images in one; and the elimination of adornments, sermonizing, and all forms of poetic filler. A corollary to his view that poetry must be purged of unnecessary embellishments was his conviction that rhyme and meter contributed little to the value of a poem.[10]

Borges was less explicit about the thematic materials that *ultraísmo* was to employ, but in general he favored contemporary rather than antique poetic furnishings. He even proclaimed that the poets of his generation preferred the beauties of a transatlantic liner or of a modern locomotive to the magnificence of Versailles or the cities of Renaissance Italy. This statement is only half-serious: what he meant was that the here and now—the immediate environment—is the logical point of departure for creating genuine lyricism and that the overuse of highly decorative trappings typical of *modernista* poetry detracted from true lyrical expression and impeded the poetic process.

At first glance, the forty-five short pieces of free verse in Borges's first collection, *Fervor de Buenos Aires* (Fervor of Buenos Aires, 1923), seem to be little more than a group of vignettes describing familiar scenes in and around his native city. A few, however, present exotic scenes: "Benarés" describes the Indian city of the same name; "Judería" ("Ghetto"), the Jewish quarter of an unspecified but obviously European city. One poem, "Rosas," takes as its point of departure the figure of Argentina's tyrannical nineteenth-century dictator. A limited number of poems are purely introspective and as such they do not describe any specific external reality. The poems vary from seven or eight lines to as many as fifty, with fifteen to twenty lines being about the average. In keeping with *ultraísta* precepts, neither regular meter, rhyme, nor regularized strophes are in evidence. The absence of traditional forms does not mean that these poems have no structure: like other writers of free verse, Borges does incorporate formal devices into his poetry. The effectiveness of these devices will be better appreciated after his poetry is examined in greater detail.

The mood of the *Fervor de Buenos Aires* is established in the opening lines of the first poem, "Las calles" (Streets):

> The streets of Buenos Aires
> have become the core of my being.
> Not the energetic streets
> troubled by haste and agitation,
> but the gentle neighborhood street
> softened by trees and twilight . . .

> Las calles de Buenos Aires
> ya son la entraña de mi alma.
> No las calles enérgicas
> molestadas de prisas y ajetreos,
> sino la dulce calle de arrabal
> enternecida de árboles y ocaso. . . .
> (*OP* 64,17)[11]

Despite the word *Fervor* in the collection's title, the reader soon becomes aware that this is a restrained fervor, a reflective passion directed toward an internalization of all that surrounds the poet. This goal is best achieved by selecting that portion of reality which is most easily assimilated: not the bustling downtown streets, but the passive, tree-shaded streets of the old suburbs. It may be a valid generalization to say that in much of his early poetry Borges sought out the passive and manageable facets of reality in order to facilitate the creation of his own internal world. A random sampling of the modifiers used in the *Fervor* bears out the point. For instance, he writes of "trees which barely mutter (their) being" ("árboles que balbucean apenas el ser"; *OP* 64,23); of the "easy tranquillity of (the) benches" ("el fácil sosiego de los bancos"; *OP* 64,26); of the "fragile new moon" ("la frágil luna nueva"; *OP* 64,43); of "withered torches" ("macilentos faroles"; *OP* 64,47); of "the obscure friendship of a vestibule" ("la amistad oscura de un zaguán"; *OP* 64,30); of the ray of light which "subdues senile easy chairs" ("humilla las seniles butacas"; *OP* 64,34) in an old parlor; and of "streets which, languidly submissive, accompany my solitude" ("calles que, laciamente sumisas, acompañan mi soledad"; *OP* 64,57). Borges's frequent use of the late afternoon as a poetic setting may have a similar function. Aside from the obvious fact that the beauty of sunsets and the coming of night have always appealed to writers, the dulling of reality's edges at this time of day gives the poet a special advantage in his task of shaping the external world.

One cannot help wondering why the young Borges felt a need to infuse reality with these qualities of passivity and submissiveness. Perhaps his innate shyness coupled with the experience of foreign travel and subsequent return to the half-familiar, half-alien scenes of his childhood led him to view the world with trepidation and a sense of insecurity. His vocabulary throughout the *Fervor* is revealing. It clearly indicates that he is seeking tranquillity, familial solidarity, and a kind of serenity that can only be associated with parental protectiveness. Examples are abundant. In "Las calles" he speaks of the neighborhood streets as providing "a promise of happiness / for under their protection so many lives are joined in brotherly love" ("una promesa de ventura / pues a su amparo hermánanse tantas vidas"; *OP* 64,17); in "Cercanías" (Environs) he writes of "neighborhoods built of quietness and tranquillity" ("arrabales hechos de acallamiento y sosiego"; *OP* 64,62); and in the beautifully understated final verses of "Un patio" he sums up the peace and serenity of the traditional Latin residence by exclaiming "How nice to live in the friendly darkness / of a vestibule, a climbing vine, of a cistern" ("Lindo es vivir en la amistad oscura / de un zaguán, de una parra y de un aljibe"; *OP* 64,30).

Closely related to Borges's poetic transmutation of "hard" reality into a pliable, manageable reality is his recourse to a certain philosophical notion that comes to occupy a central position in all his work. In "Caminata" (Stroll), one of the less anthologized poems of *Fervor*, he writes: "I am the only viewer of this street, / if I would stop looking at it, it would perish" ("Yo soy el único espectador de esta calle, / si dejara de verla se moriría"; *OP* 64,58). In "Benarés," superficially one of the least typical pieces in the collection, Borges describes in considerable detail a place he has never seen. He admits in the opening lines that the city is "False and dense / like a garden

traced on a mirror" (Falsa y tupida / como un jardín calcado en un espejo";
OP 64,53). Yet at the very end of the poem he seems amazed that the real
Benares exists: "And to think / that while I toy with uncertain metaphors, /
the city of which I sing persists" ("Y pensar / que mientras juego con
inciertas metáforas, / la cuidad que canto persiste"; OP 64,54). In a better
known poem, inspired by the Recoleta cemetery, he observes that when life
is extinguished "at the same time, space, time, and death are extinguished"
("juntamente se apagan el espacio, el tiempo, la muerte"; OP 64,20). What
Borges is driving at in these poems is made explicit in another piece,
"Amanecer" ("Daybreak"). The poem is set in the dead of night, just before
daylight appears: with "the threat of dawn" ("la amenaza del alba"), the
poet exclaims,

> I sensed the dreadful conjecture
> of Schopenhauer and Berkeley
> that declares the world
> an activity of the mind,
> a mere dream of beings,
> without basis, purpose or volume.

> Resentí la tremenda conjetura
> de Schopenhauer y de Berkeley
> que declara que el mundo
> es una actividad de la mente,
> un sueño de las almas,
> sin base ni propósito ni volumen.
>   (OP 64,47)

In the rest of the poem, Borges follows out the logic of Berkeleyan idealism.
There is a brief moment, he writes, when "only a few nightowls maintain /
and only in an ashen, sketched-out from / the vision of the streets / which
later they will, with others, define" ("sólo algunos trasnochadores conservan
/ cenicienta y apenas bosquejada / la visión de las calles / que definirán
después con los otros"; OP 64,48). In this moment in which few or no mor-
tals are maintaining the universe, "it would be easy for God / to destroy
completely his works" ("le sería fácil a Dios / matar del todo su obra!"; OP,
48). Berkeley, as a corollary to his idealism, posited God as the maintainer
of the universe—if and when there were no human beings available to perceive and hence to guarantee its existence. But Borges injects another
thought into the poem, and one that is alien to Berkeleyan philosophy. He
suggests that there is some danger that God might choose to take advantage

of this brief period when the universe hangs by a thread. The implication here is that a capricious, vindictive, or negligent God may actually wish to destroy the world. Rather than in Berkeley, the source for this notion is to be found in Gnosticism, a philosophical current that has shaped much of Borges's thought. "Amanecer," at any rate, ends on an optimistic note: dawn comes, people awake, God has not chosen to destroy the world, and "annulled night / has remained only in the eyes of the blind" ("la noche abolida / se ha quedado en los ojos de los ciegos"; *OP* 64,49).

Two of Borges's best-known essays, written years after the poetry of the *Fervor,* are intriguingly titled "Historia de la eternidad" (A history of eternity, 1936) and "Nueva refutación del tiempo" (A new refutation of time, 1947). In both these pieces, as well as in many other essays, stories, and poems, Borges's preoccupation with time is most apparent. This very human desire to halt the flow of time persisted through the last years of Borges's career, as we shall note when the poetry of the seventies and eighties is examined. Certain words and phrases that crop up in *Fervor* illustrate this intense desire. The verb *remansar* (to dam up, to create a backwater or eddy) and its related adjective *remansado* are not particularly common terms in the Spanish poetic lexicon though they appear several times in the *Fervor* and occasionally in later collections. Borges writes of an "afternoon which had been damned up into a plaza" ("la tarde toda se había remansado en la plaza"; *OP* 64, 25); of a dark, old-fashioned bedroom where a mirror is "like a backwater in the shadows" ("como un remanso en la sombra"; *OP* 64,62); of doomlike solitude "dammed-up around the town" ("La soledad . . . se ha remansado alrededor del pueblo"; *OP*64,67). The significance is obvious: if time is a river, then the poet is seeking the quiet backwaters where time's flow is halted. Though Borges's fascination with time has often been interpreted as an example of a purely intellectual exercise, the very personal sources of this interest should not be overlooked. The traumatic return to Buenos Aires as well as the essential inwardness of his personality clearly help account for the emphasis on this theme in his early work.

In addition to the *remanso* motif, the *Fervor* contains other fine examples of Borges's reaction to the rush of time. He begins the poem "Vanilocuencia" (Empty talk) by stating "the city is inside me like a poem / which I have not succeeded in stopping with words." ("La ciudad está en mí como un poema / que no he logrado detener en palabras" *OP* 64,32). Although words, especially in the form of poetry, seemingly "freeze" or "pin down" the flow of time, Borges is aware of the crushing fact that the objects of the world are "disdainful of verbal symbols" ("desdeñosas de símbolos

verbales"; *OP* 64,32) and that despite his poetry every morning he will
awake to see a new and changed world. The futility of trying to check the
flow of time by literary creations, by recalling the past, or by surrounding
oneself with old things appears clearly in the *Fervor* and subsequently became a dominant theme in all of Borges's writing. His attitude is ambivalent and leads to a poetic tension for he knows that time—in the brutally
real, everyday sense—flows on, that the world will change, that he will
grow old, and that the past is forever gone. Yet he is reluctant to give in
without a struggle, though he knows his efforts are futile. And so the rich
and plastic descriptions of antique furniture, of old photographs, and of
timeless streets are usually undermined by a word or phrase suggesting that
their solidity and apparent timelessness are merely illusory. For example, the
old daguerreotypes in "Sala vacía" ("Empty Drawing Room") are deceiving
by "their false nearness" ("su falsa cercanía"), for under close examination
they "slip away / like useless dates / of blurred anniversaries" ("se escurren
/ como fechas inútiles / de aniversarios borrosos"; *OP* 64,33). Another possible way of deceiving oneself about time, of "refuting" time, as Borges
would later say, is found in the realm of ritualistic activity. The point is well
exemplified in "El truco" (The trick), a poem whose thematic material is a
card game, but whose message is that in playing games—essentially partici-
pating in a ritual—"normal" time is displaced. He writes, "At the edges of
the card table / ordinary life is halted" ("En los lindes de la mesa / el vivir
común se detiene"; *OP* 64,27). Within the confines of the table—a magical
zone—an ancient, timeless struggle is again waged, and the "players in their
present ardor / copy the tricks of a remote age" ("los jugadores en fervor
presente / copian remotas bazas"; *OP* 64, 28). Borges concludes the poem
with the thought that this kind of activity "just barely" immortalizes the
dead comrades whose struggles are relived. For a brief moment in the heat
of the game, past and present are fused. The mythical kings, queens, and
princes whose faces decorate the "cardboard amulets" become comrades-
in-arms of the twentieth-century Argentine country folk seated about the
table.

Borges's poetry, if examined with an objective eye, reveals surprisingly
sentimental, affectionate qualities. There are, for example, some touching
love poems in *Fervor:* among these "Ausencia" (Absence), "Sábados" (Satur-
days), and "Trofeo" (Trophy) are especially noteworthy. And when Borges
writes of his favorite streets, of patios and suburban gardens, he adopts a
tone of filial devotion that suggests the warmest of personal relationships.
He displays a mood of frankness and sincerity which those who know his
work only superficially do not usually associate with him. Indeed, some of

the material in the first edition (omitted in later editions) is almost confessional in tone.[12] It seems as if the Borges of 1923 were at a crossroads. Had he been a man of different temperament, it is quite possible that he would have yielded to the temptation of creating a literature of unrestrained personal catharsis. Instead, he chose to deny the emotive side of life in his art. At least he promised that he would do this in his poetry. As he writes in one of the last poems of the *Fervor:* "I must enclose my twilight tears / within the hard diamond of a poem. / It matters not that one's soul may wander naked like the wind and alone . . ." ("He de encerrar el llanto de las tardes / en el duro diamante del poema. / Nada importa que el alma / ande sola y desnuda como el viento . . ."; *OP* 64,64)).

But Borges was not yet ready to sacrifice life and passion to art. Thus he states in the prologue to his second collection, *Luna de enfrente* (Moon across the way, 1925), that "Our daily existence is a dialogue of death and life. . . . There is a great deal of nonlife in us, and chess, meetings, lectures, daily tasks are often mere representations of life, ways of being dead."[13] He states that he wishes to avoid these "mere representations" of life in his poetry, that he prefers to write of things that affect him emotionally, of "heavenly blue neighborhood garden walls," for example. It is understandable, then, that among the twenty-eight compositions of *Luna de enfrente,* poems of deep personal involvement should predominate over pieces of a more detached and formalistic nature. A feeling of intimacy pervades the *Luna:* a third of the poems are in the second-person familiar form and the bulk of the remainder are in the first person. By contrast, the earlier *Fervor* contains only a few pieces directed to the familiar "you" (*tú*), while the majority are in the relatively impersonal third person. A further indication of the greater degree of intimacy of *Luna de enfrente* is seen in Borges's tendency to personify such inanimate things as the pampa, city streets, and the city itself. Finally, a substantial number of the compositions in the 1925 collection are love poems, among which are such memorable pieces as the "Antelación de amor" ("Anticipation of Love") and the "Dualidá en una despedida" (Duality on Saying Farewell).

Several typically Borgesian themes that appeared in *Fervor* are again seen in *Luna de enfrente.* The same tendency to soften or undermine exterior reality is evident in Borges's frequent use of the hazy light of twilight or dawn. This technique is well illustrated in such pieces as "Calle con almacén rosado" (Street with a pink store), "Dualidá en una despedida", "Montevideo," and "Ultimo sol en Villa Ortúzar" ("Sunset Over Villa Ortuzar"). Of even greater interest in the *Luna* is the poet's preoccupation with time. In this collection Borges's emphasis is on the relationship between time and memory rather than on the simple desire to halt time's flow. More precisely, memory becomes the *remanso,* the quiet backwater in which time's onward rush is checked. This relationship is very clear in "Montevideo," a poem in which Borges states that the more old-fashioned, less bustling Montevideo helps recreate the Buenos Aires of his early memories. Of the Uruguayan city he writes: "Like the memory of a frank friendship you are a clear and calm millpond in the twilight" ("Eres remansada y clara en la tarde como el recuerdo de una lisa amistad").[14] A somewhat similar verse appears in the magnificent "Anticipation of Love," when the poet describes his beloved asleep as "calm and resplendent like a bit of happiness in memory's selection" ("quieta y resplandeciente como una dicha en la selección del recuerdo"; *OP* 64,77). In these and other poems memory performs the important function of preserving past experience against the onslaught of time. But, Borges implies, memory is also a storehouse, a kind of infinite filing cabinet, the contents of which we cannot always control. We may indeed remember too much. In "Los llanos" (The plains) he writes, "It is sad that memory includes everything / and especially if memories are unpleasant" ("Es triste que el recuerdo incluya todo / y más aún si es bochornoso el recuerdo"; *OP* 64, 76). Perhaps these lines prefigure Borges's bizarre account—to be written some twenty years later—of "Funes el memorioso," the man who remembered everything.

Some two years before Borges published *Luna de enfrente* he was asked to answer a series of questions for a magazine survey of young writers. In answer to a question about his age, he wrote "I have already wearied twenty-two years."[15] The choice of words here is significant, for there is the curious tone of the world-weary old man even in his work of the mid-1920s. This tone, contrasting markedly with the passionate lyricism of several pieces in the *Luna de enfrente,* takes the form of the poet's proclaiming that he has already lived a good deal of his life and that he will do nothing new in the future. The theme is very clear in "Mi vida entera" ("My Whole Life"):

I have crossed the sea.
I have lived in many lands; I have seen one woman and two or three men
. . . I have savored many words.
I profoundly believe that this is all and that I will neither see nor do any new things.

He atravesado el mar.
He practicado muchas tierras; he visto una mujer y dos otros hombres.

. . . He paladeado numerosas palabras.
Creo profundamente que eso es todo y que ni veré ni ejecutaré cosas nuevas.

(*OP* 64, 98).

A somewhat similar tone is present in some of the poems describing the pampas: in "Los llanos," for example, Borges tries to infuse the plains with a feeling of tiredness and resignation suggestive of his own mood. It is difficult to determine what lies behind this pose of bored world-weariness. Is Borges retreating from life or is he simply stating what has become a cornerstone of his esthetic edifice: that there is nothing new under the sun; that changes, progress, novelty, and history are simply a reshuffling of a limited number of preexisting elements? Perhaps this is the philosophy he intends to set forth in the cryptic line that ends his poem "Manuscrito hallado en un libro de Joseph Conrad" ("Manuscript Found in a Book of Joseph Conrad"): "River, the first river. Man, the first man" ("El río, el primer río. El hombre, el primer hombre"; *OP* 64, 88).

Although history may be nothing more than the recurrence or the reshuffling of what has always been, Borges is nonetheless fascinated by historical events and personalities. Several of the pieces in the *Luna* show this interest. The dramatic death of the nineteenth-century gaucho leader Quiroga is very effectively commemorated in "El General Quiroga va en coche al muere" ("General Quiroga Rides to His Death in a Carriage"); the death of his own ancestor, Colonel Francisco Borges, provides the subject matter of another piece; and "Dulcia linquimus arva" evokes the early days of settlement on the pampas. Of the three, the poem to Quiroga is the most interesting for several reasons. First, the night scene of Quiroga's coach rocking across the moonlit pampa has a dramatic, almost romantic, feeling of movement uncommon in much of Borges's poetry. Second, though he is here still more or less faithful to the free verse tenets of his youth, Borges sees fit to place the poem within a fairly regular structure—rhythmic lines of about fourteen syllables arranged in quatrains having considerable assonance. The effect of this form is striking; it suggests the beat of the horses' hooves and the rocking of the coach racing on toward its encounter with destiny:

> The coach swayed back and forth rumbling the hills:
> An emphatic, enormous funeral galley.
> Four death-black horses in the darkness
> Pulled six fearful and one watchful brave man
> . . . .

That sly, trouble-making Córdoba rabble
(thought Quiroga), what power have they over me?
Here am I firm in the stirrup of life
Like a stake driven deep in the heart of the pampa. . . .

(El coche se hamacaba rezongando la altura:
un galerón enfático, enorme, funerario.
Cuatro tapaos con pinta de muerte en la negrura
tironeaban seis miedos y un valor desvelado.
. . . .
Esa cordobesada bochinchera y ladina
[meditaba Quiroga] ¿qué ha de poder con mi alma?
Aquí estoy afianzado y metido en la vida
como la estaca pampa bien metida en la pampa;
(OP 64, 80)

It is to Borges's credit as a poet that despite his mild adherence to the restrictive poetic tenets of *ultraísmo* he sensed the rightness of a more traditional form for this particular poem.

In "El General Quiroga va en coche al muere" Borges provides an insight into the kind of historical characters and events that were to dominate much of his later work, especially his prose. What fascinates him are those moments in which an individual—soldier, bandit, or similar man of action—reaches a crucial point in his life, a dramatic juncture where a turn of fate, a sudden decision, or a dazzling revelation cause a man to follow one path rather than another. Such events are delicate points of balance that determine whether a man shall become a hero or traitor, a martyr or coward. Borges was especially intrigued by them since they often provided a glimpse of an alternative track for history. What would have been the course of Argentine history if Rosas had not killed Facundo or if (as in one of his later poems) King Charles of England had not been beheaded? "General Quiroga Rides to His Death in a Carriage" is also significant in that it reveals another important side of Borges's interests. Though he may have been a shy and retiring bibliophile, he did have an undeniable affection for men of action. Gunmen, pirates, *compadres* (a kind of Buenos Aires neighborhood tough), ancient warriors, and modern spies fill the pages of his poetry, essays, and fiction.

The last group of early poems Borges chose to publish as a collection, *Cuaderno San Martín* (San Martin Notebook, 1929), contains only twelve pieces, one of which, "Arrabal en que pesa el campo" (Suburb in which the country lies heavily), has been omitted from more recent editions. Two themes dominate these poems: nostalgia for the past, and death. Often the two blend in a mood of elegiac evocation. Thus in the most memorable poems of the book Borges writes of the "mythical" founding of Buenos Aires; of his beloved Palermo district as it was at the close of the nineteenth century; of his grandfather Isidoro Acevedo; of the final resting place of his ancestors, the Recoleta cemetary; and of the suicide of his friend and fellow poet Francisco López Merino.

What the poet preserves in his memory in a sense lives; only what is gone and forgotten is really dead. In "Elegía de los portones" (Elegy to gates), for example, Borges describes the act of forgetting as "a minuscule death" ("una muerte chica"; *OP* 64, 107). Yet he is perfectly aware that death—real death—is undeniable: he knows that his attempts to negate its reality through memory and through poetry will be frustrated. He is haunted by the song of the wandering slum-minstrel in the poem to the Chacarita cemetery: "Death is life already lived. / Life is approaching death." ("La muerte es vida vivida, / la vida es muerte que viene"). It even haunts him when he writes, in the same piece, that he doesn't believe in the cemetery's decrepitude and that "the fullness of only one rose is greater than all your tombstones" ("la plenitud de una sola rosa es más que tus mármoles"; *OP* 64, 122).

One of the most interesting pieces in the collection is on the death of Borges's ancestor, Isidoro Acevedo. Aside from its intrinsic value, this poem is noteworthy because in it Borges gives a clear hint of the kind of literature he would produce in the decade to follow. This "prefiguring"—to use one of his own favorite terms—of his future prose occurs in the description of Acevedo's last day. The old man lying on his deathbed in a state of feverish delirium plans a complete military compaign in his mind. Though Acevedo only mutters a few fragmentary phrases, Borges uses these as a point of departure to recreate the very concrete fantasy he assumes his moribund grandfather was in effect experiencing:

He dreamt of two armies
that were going into the shadows of battle;
he enumerated each commanding officer, the banners, each unit
. . . .
He surveyed the pampa
noted the rough country that the infantry might seize
and the smooth plain in which a cavalry strike would be invincible.
He made a final survey,

he gathered together the thousands of faces that man unknowingly knows after
  many years:
bearded faces that are probably fading away in daguerreotypes,
faces that lived near his own in Puente Alsina and Cepeda.
. . . .
He gathered an army of Buenos Aires' ghosts . . .
. . . .
He died in the military service of his faith in the *patria*.

Soñó con dos ejércitos
que entraban en la sombra de una batalla;
enumeró los comandos, las banderas, las unidades.
. . . .
Hizo leva de pampa:
vió terreno quebrado para que pudiera aferrarse la infantería
y llanura resuelta para que el tirón de la caballería fuera invencible.
Hizo una leva última,
congregó los miles de rostros que el hombre sabe sin saber después de los años:
caras de barba que se estarán desvaneciendo en daguerrotipos,
caras que vivieron junto a la suya en el Puente Alsina y Cepeda.
. . . .
juntó un ejército de sombras porteñas
. . . .
murió en milicia de su convicción por la patria.

(OP 64, 113–14)

Those who are familiar with Borges's fiction may appreciate the similarity
of this poem to such short stories as the "Ruinas circulares" ("The Circular
Ruins"). There are only a few steps between describing the disturbing concreteness of dreams and suggesting that what we call the real world may actually be the product of some unknown being's dream.

Borges continued to write poetry after 1929, though his output of verse,
particularly during the thirties and forties, was not very great. There may be
some significance to the fact that between the summer of 1929 and the
spring of 1931 he published nothing. This hiatus may have been due to the
extremely unsettled political and economic conditions of the period: a similar pattern can be observed in the literary activity of other Argentine writers
during the same two years. When Borges resumed publishing, he devoted
himself chiefly to essays and literary criticism, genres in which he had been
working steadily throughout the twenties. It was not until 1934 that he
again began writing poetry. Oddly enough, he broke his poetic silence with
two pieces composed in English. These were followed by "Insomnio" (In-

somnia, 1936), "La noche cíclica" ("The Cyclical Night," 1940), "Del infierno y del cielo" (Of heaven and hell, 1942), "Poema conjectural" ("Conjectural poem," 1943), and "Poema del cuarto elemento" (Poem of the fourth element, 1944). Between March 1944 and April 1953 Borges wrote no poetry; at least he published none. Yet it was during this period that he produced his most celebrated stories and a number of important essays. The seven poems that Borges published between 1934 and 1944 are, at first glance, quite dissimilar in both form and content. The "Two English Poems," for example, are amorous in theme and are cast in extremely free verse, so much so that they could be regarded as poetic prose:

> I offer you my ancestors, my dead men; the ghosts
> that living men have honoured in marble:
> my father's father killed in the frontier of
> Buenos Aires, two bullets through his lungs,
> bearded and dead, wrapped by his soldiers in
> the hide of a cow; my mother's grandfather
> —just twenty-four—heading a charge of
> three hundred men in Peru, now ghosts on vanished horses."
>
> (*OP* 64, 142)

"Insomnio" is also written in free verse, but unlike the "Two English Poems" its lines are generally shorter and its appearance on the printed page is more traditional. "La noche cíclica," in sharp contrast to most of the poetry Borges had published previously, is written in neat quatrains rhymed in the *cuarteto* pattern (abba). In the next two poems of this group, "Del infierno y del cielo" and "Conjectural Poem," Borges reverted to a rather free unrhymed form, only to use the *cuarteto* again in 1944 in his "Poema del cuarto elemento." The significance of these formal shifts should not be overestimated: they only indicate that Borges would from this point on be bound neither by the orthodoxy of his free-verse *ultraísta* years nor by the orthodoxy of traditional forms.

Why Borges chose to write the "Two English Poems" in the language of his paternal grandmother is a matter neither he nor his commentators have discussed. Perhaps these compositions are merely a tour de force or perhaps they indicate a feeling of alienation from the not too pleasant surroundings of Buenos Aires in the early thirties. Certain details in the poems suggest the latter possibility. Borges reveals an ennui and desperation in these pieces that are clearly lacking in the earlier poetry. The opening lines of the first poem are indicative of this mood: "The useless dawn finds me in a deserted

street corner." A bit later he speaks of the night as having left him "some
hated friends to chat / with, music for dreams, and the smoking of / bitter
ashes. The things that my hungry heart / has no use for." The piece ends on
a note of great intensity summed up in some of Borges's finest lines. At daybreak, the poet says, "The shattering dawn finds me in a deserted street of
my city." The "lazily and incessantly beautiful" woman to whom the poem
is addressed is gone. The poet is left with only memories of the encounter
and with a desperate longing: "I must get at you, somehow: I put away
those / illustrious toys you have left me, I want your hidden look, your real
smile—that lonely, / mocking smile your cool mirror knows" (OP 64, 140–
41). The same tone of desperation pervades the second English poem when
the poet asks his beloved:

> What can I hold you with?
> I offer you lean streets, desperate sunsets, the
> moon of jagged suburbs.
> I offer you the bitterness of a man who has looked
> long and long at the lonely moon.

Throughout the remainder of the piece—as quotable as any Borges has
written—he continues to enumerate what he can "offer." The last lines reinforce and climax the entire poem: "I can give you my loneliness, my darkness, the / hunger of my heart; I am trying to bribe you / with uncertainty,
with danger, with defeat" (OP 64, 142–43). The details of these give a pic-
ture of almost surrealistic disintegration: *lean* streets, *shattering dawn, jag-
ged* suburbs. These are not typically Borgesian adjectives. And in
"Insomnio," a poem whose intent is admittedly quite different from that of
the English pieces, the poet's restlessness is aggravated by visions of "shattered tenements" ("despedazado arrabal"), "leagues of obscene garbage-
strewn pampa" ("leguas de pampa basurera y obscena", and similar scenes
(OP 64, 138).

The references to insomnia, to loneliness, to bitterness, and the use of adjectives suggestive of disintegration have little in common with the often ardent, though seldom desperate, poems of the earlier collections. The
unusual character of his verse of the thirties points to the fact that he was
undergoing a period of transition in his literary career. Borges seems, moreover, to have suffered some kind of personal crisis, aggravated, perhaps, by a
political and economic environment distasteful to him. An examination of
his prose of the mid-1930s supports this view. It is especially significant

that the genesis of his distinctive fiction—a literature of evasion, his critics might say—comes precisely at this time.

Early Essays and Criticism

Before coming to grips with Borges's most central work, the prose fiction of the forties and fifties, we must examine his early essayistic writing. His activity in this area began at almost the same time that he started writing poetry. Not surprisingly, his earliest essays often reflect the preoccupations of a poet: notes on fellow poets, the nature of imagery, and comments on literary movements. Other concerns, however, appear early, though the connection with literature is almost always evident. Philosophic questions, Argentine culture, and his immediate Buenos Aires surroundings all seem to fascinate him. In retrospect, however, it seems clear that the most significant essayistic texts of the period all deal with literature in one way or another. While Borges's comments on philosophers like Berkeley or Schopenhauer are interesting and do shed some light on his own writing, they are hardly original. Indeed his struggles with the concept of time, for example, do not go much beyond the ideas of Heraclitus (one of his favorites), who reminded us in the fifth century B.C. that "one cannot step twice into the same river." In short, philosophic notions were fascinating intellectual toys for Borges and the literary games that he played with them enliven his texts, but he was no philosopher. Similarly, his essays on Argentine character, *barrio* life, folk heroes, and the like relate nicely to the thematic concerns of his poetry and later prose fiction, but of themselves are not the stuff that makes for an internationally recognized man of letters. The situation is different, however, when his literary essays are considered. Although Borges cannot be viewed as a systematic literary critic, his miscellaneous notes, comments, and essays on literature, together with the models he provided in his creative texts, have had a marked impact upon contemporary literary theory, as will be noted later in this study.

Borges's essayistic work consists of some half dozen early collections and several more recent volumes of mixed-genre pieces. The formal classification of many individual items is problematic in that they range from genuine essays to short parablelike musings, to texts that either combine narratives within an essayistic framework or present essayistic material within a narrative. Moreover, if one were to accept a very broad definition of the essay genre, a number of texts usually considered as prose fiction might be viewed as essentially essayistic. Parenthetically, Borges's blurring of traditional generic boundaries, his experiments with hybrid literary forms (What do we call a book review of a nonexistent book?) is a fascinating topic; it is, moreover, consistent with the "postmodernist" tag occasionally accorded him.

In assessing Borges's total production of nonfictional prose one should not lose sight of the great range covered by his writing and of the fact that a great deal of his more popular work has never been reprinted in his essay collections. For each one of his well-known, sophisticated, and highly intellectualized essays, he has written many unpretentious and informative book reviews. During the late thirties, for example, his column "Libros y autores extranjeros" (Foreign books and authors) in the popular magazine *El Hogar* gave the average Argentine reader an appetizing taste of many relatively unknown literary delights. His work as a reviewer for such publications as *Sur* and the *Anales de Buenos Aires* during the forties was also noteworthy. Nor should Borges's contributions as an editor and writer of prologues be overlooked in surveying his nonfictional prose. His anthologies of fantastic fiction (done in collaboration with Silvina Ocampo and Adolfo Bioy Casares) and of detective stories (in collaboration with Bioy Casares) were widely circulated. Borges wrote introductions and prologues for dozens of books, many of them translations of such celebrated American authors as William Faulkner, Henry James, and Bret Harte. He also collaborated in the preparation of several anthologies of Argentine literature and, in 1951, wrote (with Delia Ingenieros) a guide to *Antiguas literaturas germánicas*. These far-ranging writings, while not of primary interest in our analysis of Borges's literary trajectory, do help refute the charges that have occasionally been made that he was an intellectual snob and strictly "a writer's writer." Borges may well have been an extremely bookish person, but he nonetheless wished to share the adventure, excitement, and pleasures of good reading with a large audience. In short, when his total activity is weighed, his role as a literary popularizer and mentor must be taken into consideration.

Borges's first book of essays, *Inquisiciones* (Inquisitions, 1925), is dominated by pieces dealing with poetic theory and, by extension, the nature of language itself, along with a few essays reflecting his philosophic interests. In several pieces he discusses literary *criollismo,* his deep affection for his native city, the relationship of the pampa to Buenos AIres, and the work of such compatriots as the poet Lugones and the novelist Güiraldes. In addition to these themes, the collection includes essays on foreign literary works and authors: *The Thousand and One Nights,* Quevedo, Edward Fitzgerald, and others—interests that would be reflected in Borges's work for years to come. Despite an occasional barb, most of the essays are not polemical in tone. Its strong title not withstanding, these are gentle "inquisitions" in which Borges prefers the role of observer to that of preceptor.

There are two essays in *Inquisiciones* that merit special attention: "La nadería de la personalidad" (The nothingness of personality) and "La encrucijada de Berkeley" (Berkeley's turning point). Both are philosophical rather than literary, both are sketchy formulations of ideas that were to dominate much of Borges's later work, and both were inspired by conversations with one of his most influential early mentors, the eccentric, little-known writer Macedonia Fernández.[16] In the first of these pieces Borges tries to show how the *yo*, the ego, as a discrete, identifiable entity has no reality. Ideas from Buddhism, Agrippa, and Schopenhauer are brought to bear on the central theme. In some mystical sense, Borges (under the spell, no doubt, of Macedonia Fernández) agrees with Agrippa that the individual who attempts to express himself "wants to express life in its entirety."[17] There is a quality of "allness" in the ego: perhaps what Borges is saying may be reduced to the familiar notion of the ego as a microcosm of the universe. Toward the end of the essay, he seems to be especially attracted to Schopenhauer's idea of the ego as simply an "immovable point" that may serve as a vantage point from which to determine the flight of time. Viewed as a whole, the ideas in the essay do not fall into a clear or philosophically rigorous pattern, yet they do show a number of Borgesian themes in embryonic form. The microcosm idea, the notion of an entire life or an entire universe being compressed into one point in space appears frequently in other texts—for instance, in "El Aleph" ("The Aleph") and in "La esfera de Pascal" ("The Fearful Sphere of Pascal"), among others. The nothingness of the individual ego, along with the corresponding idea that the one is the all, were later to be expanded by Borges into themes of ambivalent personality, duplicated personality, and the like.

A good part of the "Encrucijada de Berkeley" consists of a rather routine sketch of the philosopher's essential ideas. Yet Borges, like many writers since Berkeley's time, wonders how the existence of mind itself can be posited if, in the Berkeleyan sense, it is the very means by which the entire universe exists. Borges appears to be dissatisfied with his understanding of the subtleties of this philosophic system. Thus, while the ideas of Berkeleyan idealism obviously fascinate him, he quite honestly writes that they are "more readily stated than understood."[18] This confession is significant: Borges made no pretense to being a philosopher, yet he was very much attracted by the outward form of philosophic notions. Moreover, the fact that he may not have thoroughly understood a particular concept did not inhibit his manipulating the concept in his literature. Witness the frequent touches of Berkeleyan idealism in his early poetry at a time when he clearly admits that he possessed more of a verbal familiarity with this philosophy than a genuine comprehension of it. Perhaps Borges has done what many of us do: perhaps he seized upon ideas only dimly seen, but by constantly using them, by accepting them *as if* he understood them profoundly, they became in a very real sense thoroughly learned.

In *El tamaño de mi esperanza* (The size of my hope, 1926) Borges continues to pursue several of the themes announced in *Inquisiciones:* the analysis of poetic language and especially the nature of *criollismo,* the nation's essence as expressed in its culture, especially literature. In discussing such figures as Sarimento, Del Campo, Lugones, and Carriego, he stresses the need for authenticity rather than the merely picturesque. In retrospect, some of the most fascinating passages in these essays appear to be almost parenthetical remarks. This is well illustrated in a rather rambling text, "Profesión de fe literaria" (A profession of literary faith), in which Borges casually presents an idea that was to become central to his view of literary art. Variety, he notes, is a specious quality, and only a few words or a few pages really matter to any writer. Borges presents, in effect, a good defense against the criticism that he frequently reworks themes, ideas, and even specific pages of earlier writings. If his ideas on variety are extended slightly, his views on literary originality may be better appreciated. Writers have a limited number of valid themes available to them, and literature may be conceived of as a finite body of material that the world's authors have reshuffled and rearranged; hence, originality itself becomes a questionable myth and to consider it the defining quality of good writing is untenable. Moreover, Borges was surprisingly sensitive to the fact that many writers (perhaps himself) occasionally repeat themselves or rework older material. In his very favorable review of Shaw's *St. Joan,* for example, he remarks "I haven't come upon the slightest bit of self-plagiarism, a thing at which my poverty is amazed."[19] The reference to his own "poverty" may be significant: it indicated that Borges, even in 1926, feared that the range of his own literary talents was somewhat limited.

Perhaps the most significant essay of the collection is "Palabrería para versos" (Wordiness for verses) in that it deals with the difficult and fundamental question of the relationship of words to things. Borges makes one point in this essay that must be underscored. He notes that the single word is a kind of shorthand, an arbitrary summing-up of complex impressions. By way of example he cites such ordinary nouns as "orange," "dagger," or "afternoon" and shows how each could be described by a lengthy circumlocution rather than by the conventional one-word term. It is a philosophical and linguistic commonplace to state that language may be described as an arbitrary set of symbols that do not have a one-for-one relationship to bits of clearly defined absolute reality, and this is essentially what Borges is saying. But taken in the context of his literary development these ideas are very important. They foreshadow his interest in the philosophy of nominalism and they help explain some of the intricacies encountered by those readers of his fiction who journey with him to the strange world of Tlön.

Like his other early essay collections, *El tamaño de mi esperanza* is valuable to the student of Borges's literary trajectory in that it indicates what books he was reading and what ideas were coming to dominate his thought. In addition to the interest in the symbolic aspect of language, the genesis of another one of his philosophical concerns can be seen in the essay "Historia de los ángeles" (A history of angels). Borges had a consistent interest in Judaic culture—perhaps because of personal contacts with the large Buenos Aires Jewish community, perhaps because of a close boyhood friend during his stay in Switzerland, perhaps because of some sentimental attachment stemming from the fact that he had some distant Jewish antecedents, or simply because he appreciated the rich intellectual contributions of this people. At any rate, both his poetry and prose give evidence of a surprisingly broad knowledge of Jewish folkways, traditions, and literature. The "Historia de los ángeles" is actually an extended book review of two volumes, John Peter Stehelin's *Rabbinical Literature* and Erich Bischoff's *Elements of the Kabala*. The latter is the more important of the two because it shows Borges's early fascination with Jewish mysticism, numerology, and the like. Typically Kabalistic notions—the secret revelations of numerical relations, the world as a hidden cipher, and the mystic power of a code word—have played an especially important part in Borges's fiction, as readers of "The Aleph" or "La muerte y la brújula" ("Death and the Compass") soon discover; however, at this point in his literary development these ideas, like those on the nature of language, are in fragmentary form. They should be thought of as mere bits of "mental idlenesses," a phrase that Borges, in his characteristically offhand manner, used to describe this entire collection.

Two volumes conclude Borges's prose production of the decade: an essay collection *El idioma de los argentinos* (The language of the Argentines, 1928) and an essayistic biography, *Evaristo Carriego* (1930). Both are similar to the earlier collections in mood and content, and for those interested in literary biography they are especially rich. For example, in one essay of *El idioma,* "La fruición literaria" (Literary fruition), the young Borges reveals his favorite readings since childhood—a fascinating catalogue of works ranging from Greek mythology to the Argentine "dime novels" of Eduardo Gutiérrez, and including such favorites as Quevedo, Carlyle, Schopenhauer, Unamuno, Dickens, Verne, and the ever present *Thousand and One Nights*. A casual remark near the end of the essay is perhaps as revealing of Borges as the specific works themselves. He candidly remarks of the favorite books, "I reread them with fond recollection, and new readings do not arouse my enthusiasm."[20] This comment by a man of twenty-nine reveals his essential conservatism. The tendency to return to well-worn themes and to familiar writers, his reservations regarding originality and novelty, and his fascination with the notion of repetition are all facets of this same essential characteristic.

An unimportant-looking piece, buried amidst the impressive and sophisticated literary criticism of the other essays in the *Idioma de los argentinos*, bears out this view of Borges extremely well. In the first place, it shows in a dramatic, almost poetic manner the author's obsessive desire to negate the flow of time. Second, it demonstrates Borges's tendency to reinsert a favorite page into later writings that deal with similar themes. It is almost as if Borges were trying to show his personal adherence to the idea that there is nothing new under the sun. Titled "Sentirse en muerte" (A sense of death) in this collection, this piece reappears in the text of the title essay of the collection *Historia de la eternidad* (A history of eternity, 1936) and again is intercalated into his essay of 1947, *Nueva refutación del tiempo* (A new refutation of time). With characteristic candor, Borges tells us in these later works that the piece dates from 1928. At the start of "Sentirse en muerte" Borges explains that there may be some readers who will understand his arguments on time and eternity more easily through his recounting a personal experience than by means of a technical philosophical presentation. What he retells in the essay will be familiar to many. He recalls strolling one evening through a neighborhood of Buenos Aires he seldom frequented. Struck by the humble yet charming sight of typically old-fashioned houses, surrounded by gardens and fig trees, Borges pauses to drink in the stillness of moonlight, the arched doorways and garden walls: "I remained staring at this simplicity. I thought, surely out loud: this is the same as thirty years ago. . . . The facile thought that I am somewhere in the nineteenth century ceased to be a few approximate words and was deepened into reality. I felt dead, I felt that I was an abstract spectator of the world. . . . I did not think that I had returned upstream on the so-called waters of Time; rather I suspected that I was the possessor of an illusive or absent sense of the inconceivable world eternity. Only later did I succeed in defining that imagination."[21] The importance of "Sentirse en muerte" lies in the fact that it is the earliest expression in prose of a key Borgesian theme, one that had already figured prominently in his poetry of the twenties. It points up his growing tendency to intellectualize in prose rather than simply to express essentially poetic insights in verse.

It has already been noted that the mid-1930s may mark a turning point, if not a crisis, in Borges's life as a writer. The changes in his poetry and the ensuing decrease in his production of verse suggest this as do the essays in *Discusión* (Discussion, 1932). Yet it would be incorrect to claim that a "new" Borges emerges during this period, for his essential preoccupations and his basic literary outlook remain what they were in the twenties. What changes is Borges's emphasis and to a degree his manner of expression. The intellectualization—hinted at in earlier essays—now comes out in full flower; his tendency to escape the here and the now through memory and poetic evocation gives way to a greater interest in the arcane, the esoteric, and the exotic.

Indicative of these new interests was his growing fascination with the cosmology and metaphysics of the ancient Gnostics, topics that he had touched upon earlier but that became a central concern in his essay "Una vindicación del falso Basilides" (A vindication of the false Basilides). With typical frankness he begins the piece by telling his readers exactly how he first became interested in this unusual philosophy. As a youth of seventeen, he happened upon Quevedo's work on the Gnostic heresies; shortly afterward, while in Europe, he read the German version of George Mead's rich anthology of Gnostic thought, *Fragments of a Faith Forgotten,* as well as various encyclopedia articles. This philosophical tradition is too vast, too complex, and too varied to be outlined here: those who would like to follow its threads through Borges's prose might profit by reading Mead's volume, apparently his main source of information. Among the intricacies of Gnosticism several ideas seem to hold a special fascination for him: the notion of a creator "behind" the creator, with the implication that the God of the main Judeo-Christian tradition is merely an "intermediary," a much lesser being—perhaps even the adversary of the true Master; the concept of an almost infinite number of angels, gods, demigods, and intermediaries inhabiting the cosmos; the suggestion of a creator behind a creator, behind a creator, and so on; the notion of a multiplicity of possible worlds; and finally, the view of the world's coming into existence quite haphazardly, as the mere whim of a "minor" creator.

"Una vindicación de la Cábala" (A vindication of the Kabala), written in 1931 and included in *Discusión,* may be thought of as a companion piece to the essay on Basilides in that the roots of both the Kabala and the gnosis are intimately entwined in the mystery cults of the ancient Near East. Despite its title, the piece deals more with a cabalistic approach to Christian Scripture than it does with the content of this famous compendium of Hebraic numerology, mysticism, and ancient lore. Borges focuses his attention upon the problem of the exact meaning of the Trinity and especially upon the significance of the words "Holy Ghost." He conjectures that the phrase may be merely a syntactical form and that "what is certain is that the third blind person of the tangled trinity is the recognized author of the Scriptures."[22] If this is so, Borges continues, the Scriptures are indeed "dictated"; they are complete, and contain no gratuitous or chance elements. At the essay's conclusion Borges further hypothesizes that if we grant this completeness and the necessity of every scriptural detail, then we might find, by applying the cabalistic method of treating divine writing as a code, that every detail, every word, every number in the Scriptures has a secret, unrevealed meaning. Curiously, the essay ends abruptly at this point.

Borges's interest in Judaic literature, particularly in its more mystical manifestations, was to reappear many times again in his work. In another essay of *Discusión,* "El otro Whitman" (The other Whitman), he tries to characterize the breadth, the all-encompassing quality of the North American's poetry by citing a passage from the Hebrew *Zohar* in which the vastness and omnipresence of God is described. And in his fiction such famous pieces as "El milagro secreto" ("The Secret Miracle") and "Death and the Compass" attest to his great fascination with Judaic culture.

In addition to these essays, *Discusión* is rich in texts illustrative of Borges's literary and philosophic world. The collection's concluding piece, "La perpetua carrera de Aquiles y la tortuga" (The perpetual race of Achilles and the tortoise), deals with the notion of infinitude and is frequently cited as an early example of Borges's preoccupation with this concept. But in the light of present-day critical thinking the literary essays in the collection seem to be of even greater significance. Of these, "El arte narrativo y la magia" (Narrative art and magic) is especially interesting because it gives us a good idea of the underlying narrative theory that was soon to infuse Borges's first fictional pieces. He begins the essay by discussing Poe, William Morris, and Melville. He states that what he likes in these authors is the "secret plot," the arcane element that one may discover in their work. In contrast to the work of these few writers, much of the typical fiction of the same period—the mid-nineteenth century—falls into the category of "the draggy novel of characters" (*D,* 88), whereas the ideal novel should be "a precise game of staying on the alert, of echoes, and of affinities" (*D,* 90). Borges points out an example of this kind of fiction in a story of Chesterton and then sums up the alternatives with which any writer of narrative fiction is faced: "I have contrasted two causal processes: the natural one, which is the incessant result of uncontrollable and infinite operations; [and] the lucid and limited magical one, wherein the details are prophetic. In the novel, I feel that the only possible honesty lies in the second alternative. Leave the first to psychological fakery" (D, 91).

The full impact of this sweeping division of novelists into sheep and goats, which this statement implies, may be difficult to appreciate at first glance. Borges is in effect saying that the "psychological" novel, and all fiction that develops its structure from the interplay of personalities (personality viewed in toto), should be relegated to the category of "fakery." He holds, and with some justification, that the infinitude of events, causal factors, "influences," and the like which constitute a single human life are so complex that the writer who attempts to build a work of fiction on such material is pretentious and dishonest. Rather, he suggests that writers abandon attempts at psychological realism in fiction, limit their material, organize it, and emphasize the narrative element by structuring detail to fit a preconceived (perhaps even a secret, "held-back") pattern. In a word, novelists should aim at producing "a precise game of staying on the alert, of echoes and affinities." Borges thus presents a manifesto of prose fiction, and a defense of his own, but as yet unwritten, work in the genre. The essay may also help explain why a substantial number of his early readers and critics, especially devotees of psychological literature, could not accept Borges as a great prose writer.

The ironically titled *Historia de la eternidad* (A history of eternity, 1936), Borges's next prose collection, contains only six pieces. One of these, the "El acercamiento a Almotásim" ("The Approach to al-Mu'tasim"), poses interesting problems of generic classification, but is usually treated as an example of his fiction. The title essay is Borges's longest effort in the genre. In it he devotes some forty pages to a compilation of his ideas on the flow of time, Berkeleyian idealism, and the meaning of eternity. Despite its length, or perhaps because of it, the essay seems less appealing than some of his other writings on the subject. In "Historia de la eternidad," moreover, Borges makes rather generous use of materials drawn from earlier essays: thus a section of "Una vindicación de la Cábala" (A vindication of the Cabala) reappears as does the complete "Sentirse en muerte."

Of the remaining essays in the collection several are sufficiently important to be noted in a general study of his work. "La doctrina de los ciclos" (The doctrine of the cycles) is especially interesting because it touches upon a key Borgesian theme, the relation of time and infinity. He begins the piece by examining such mathematical and physical concepts as the laws of thermodynamics and the idea of entropy. Borges comes to the conclusion that if we have a universe with finite matter and infinite time, sooner or later things get back to a "repeated" state and that then the cycle begins to work itself out once again. He concludes this rather complex essay by noting that there is no "practical" concern in all this. Though this observation may be correct, the essay is noteworthy because it sheds light on such pieces as the poem "The Cyclical Night" or the story "La biblioteca de Babel" ("The Library of Babel"), both of which are based on the same central idea. Another piece in the collection, "Las kenningar" (The Kenningar), is significant in that it indicates an early interest in ancient Nordic folk literature, a subject that was to become an almost obsessive theme in Borges's later work.

The forties was, as we shall see, a time of intense literary activity for Borges. Not only did he publish his most celebrated prose fiction during the period, but he also produced a number of essays that have achieved canonical status. These texts are found in the collection *Otras inquisiciones* (*Other Inquisitions*, 1952) and in the individually published essay "Nueva refutación del tiempo" (A new refutation of time, 1947). The latter merits fairly detailed analysis. Borges explains in the prologue to the essay that it is in two parts, the first half of which appeared in *Sur* in 1944. He admits that in the present day his ideas are an "anachronous *reductio ad absurdum* of a preterite system."[23] He also notes that the very title contains a logical fallacy, for how can time be "refuted" when the temporal term "new" is used in reference to the word "time"? Borges's essential candor is again seen in the first paragraph of the essay when he says that in the course of his life "I have perceived . . . a refutation of time, in which I myself disbelieve, but which comes to visit me at night and in the weary dawns with the illusory force of an axiom" (*OI*, 172). He then notes some of the many places in his writings where this obsessive desire to refute time comes to the surface, though he discerningly points out that in "some way or another" it is to be found in all his books. Yet he openly states that he is not satisfied with his previous attempts to set forth the refutation. He characterizes his most ambitious attempt in this direction, the *Historia de la eternidad,* as "less demonstrative and reasoned than divinatory and pathetic"—a singularly honest evaluation with which many will be forced to agree.

The "New Refutation" is written in a closely knit and rigorous style. It admits little condensation and should be read in its entirety. At the risk of doing the essay and Borges an injustice, a few salient points may, however, be extracted. The first of these is that once we accept the negation of the "continuities" of matter, spirit, and space, it follows that the continuity of time may be—or must be—negated. The route by which Borges leads his reader through Berkeley and Hume to this point is strewn with rocks and confused by such intersecting side roads as the one marked "Schopenhauer's dualism: Do not enter." To reinforce his negation of time's continuity, Borges resorts to a number of commonsense arguments, the bulk of which revolve about the idea that two events occurring at what we would call the same moment in time may only be "contemporary" in historical retrospect. When Borges's ancestor Captain Isidoro Suárez was leading an attack in Peru early in August 1824, De Quincey was publishing a book in London. The two men died in complete ignorance of each other. These and other examples lead Borges to ask, "if time is a mental process, how can it be shared by thousands, or even two different men?" (*OI*, 177) At the close of the first part of the essay (the section written in 1944), Borges, as always desperately trying to convince himself and his reader of something in which he admittedly "does not believe," employs two tactics. He first absolves himself for not being able to communicate his analysis of time on the ground that language is by its very nature an inadequate instrument for the discussion of time, and second, he makes a last-ditch attempt at getting his point over by reprinting—once again—the "Sentirse en muerte" fragment of 1928.

The second section (text "B") of the "New Refutation" was written in 1947, some three years after the first part. Borges explains that in it he wishes to do exactly what he wished to do in the first part but that he deliberately did not fuse the two essays into one, because "the reading of two similar texts could facilitate the understanding of an indocile subject" (*OI*, 172). Thus "B" follows the same general lines as the earlier text: Berkeleyan idealism is again explained, and its misinterpretations noted. Borges places considerable emphasis on extending Hume's idea—also implicit in Berkeley—that the self can be considered a bundle or collection of different perceptions that succeed each other with inconceivable rapidity. In his attempt to deny the existence of time, or perhaps in his desire to redefine it as merely the consciousness of the present moment, Borges tries to manipulate Hume's denial of the metaphysical notion of "self" and to incorporate into his own thinking the same philosopher's concept of time as "a succession of indivisible moments." But as in text "A" of the essay, both author and reader seem to become hopelessly entangled in this finespun reasoning.

An important difference in the 1947 portion of the essay as compared with the earlier text is in the choice of exemplary material. In text "B" Borges uses the ancient Chinese tale of Chuang Tzu, the man who dreamt

he was a butterfly and upon waking did not know if he was indeed a man
who had dreamt he was a butterfly or a butterfly who was now dreaming
that he was a man. He also employs certain figurative passages from Budd-
hist literature, as well as miscellaneous quotations from Plutarch,
Schopenhauer, and F. H. Bradley. All point to the reality of the present moment and to the logical necessity of denying the existence of past or future.
Though all these arguments are far from convincing, the essay's last paragraph is one of the most quotable Borges has ever written. Its ironies can,
perhaps, only be appreciated after one has fought along with Borges in this
magnificent and futile struggle:

And yet, and yet—To deny temporal succession, to deny the ego, to deny the astro-
nomical universe, are apparent desperations and secret assuagements. Our destiny
(unlike the hell of Swedenborg and the hell of Tibetan mythology) is not horrible
because of its unreality; it is horrible because it is irreversible and ironbound. Time
is the substance I am made of. Time is a river that carries me away, but I am the
river; it is a tiger that mangles me, but I am the tiger; it is a fire that consumes me,
but I am the fire. The world, alas, is real; I, alas, am Borges. (*OI*, 186–87)

Other Inquisitions contains many essays dealing with great writers and
their works: old favorites such as Chesterton, Quevedo, Whitman, and
Cervantes along with several less frequented figures such as Coleridge,
Kafka, Hawthorne, and Valéry. Not surprisingly several of these texts illuminate some of Borges's most basic literary tenets. Perhaps the most
provocative essays in the volume are focused on the nature of the novel, a
genre that Borges himself never cultivated. It will be recalled that he had
already discussed certain aspects of prose fiction in 1932 in "El arte
narrativo y la magia." Several of his uncollected pieces help round out his
views on narration, plot structure, and the like. In one of these, a book review of Faulkner's *Absalom, Absalom!* he pays the North American novelist high tribute by noting that he (like Joseph Conrad) has the rare talent
of being on the one hand "profoundly human" and, on the other, of being
a "pure" artist in the sense that his "central concern is for verbal proce-
dures." Most important, Borges reveals a critical attitude toward the very
successful novelist who is not much concerned with formal structure, but
whose work is based simply on "the passions and doings of man." This
kind of writer, he observes, is "more fortunate and knows the laudatory
epithets 'profound,' 'human,' 'profoundly human.'"[24] A newspaper review of Hugh Walpole's murder mystery *The Killer and the Slain* sheds
more light on his attitude toward the novel. In this piece he again reveals

his fondness for detective fiction and similarly highly structured narratives; but the most interesting part of the review comes when Borges applies to novels Edgar Allan Poe's idea that there is really no such thing as a "long poem": "this argument is transferable to prose and it could be reasoned that the novel is not a literary genre but rather a mere typographical phantom."[25]

When Borges questions the very existence of the genre, he shows, although in an exaggerated way, his low evaluation of a great many highly regarded novels of the modern period. His preferences in longer prose fiction are for allegory, romance, and, of course, the detective tale. Thus in *Other Inquisitions* he seems to take almost perverse pleasure in writing glowingly of William Beckford's *Vathek,* a rather obscure Gothic novel known chiefly to students of eighteenth-century letters. On the other hand, he either ignores or treats casually many of the major novelists of the past two centuries. Even when he discusses an important novelist, he tends to praise their lesser-known compositions or subtle details in their major works. In his essay on Hawthrone—given first as a lecture in 1949 but included in *Other Inquisitions*—he notes that the American writer devises situations first and then lets his characters in a sense "play out" the roles demanded by the situation. This method, he states "can produce . . . admirable stories . . . but not admirable novels" (*OI,* 53). Hence, he apparently prefers Hawthorne's short fiction, for example, a story such as "Wakefield" rather than *The Scarlet Letter* or *The House of Seven Gables.* Borges's penchant for praising an unusual detail in a well-known work is especially evident in his comments on *Don Quijote.* Rather than the broad human sweep of Cervantes' masterpiece, what he decides to discuss is the fact that Don Quijote himself (in the ninth chapter) reads the *Don Quijote.* Thus in "Magias parciales del Quijote" ("Partial Magic in the Quixote") he playfully observes, "these inversions suggest that if the characters in a story can be readers or spectators, than we, their readers or spectators can be fictitious" (*OI,* 46). In several other essays in *Other Inquisitions* Borges reveals his strong opinions on the novel, for instance, in "De las alegorías a las novelas" ("From Allegories to Novels"), in which he discusses the modern shift away from allegory by contrasting the ideas of Croce and Chesteron, in his essays on Wells, Kafka, or Chesterton, and elsewhere. One of his clearest, most provocative denunciations of the modern novel, and indeed of most contemporary literature, appears in the "Nota sobre (hacia) Bernard Shaw" ("For Bernard Shaw"). Significantly, Shaw, whom he praises highly, is not a novelist. Borges tells us that Shaw, like the poet Valéry, who is also lauded in *Other Inquisitions,* is one of the few moderns who has not surrendered to the "immoral" cult of sentimentality, desperation, anguish, and existentialism. The eloquent and lucid final paragraph of "For Bernard Shaw" bears citing in its entirety:

> Man's character and its variations constitute the essential theme of the novel of our time; lyric poetry is the complacent magnification of amorous fortunes or misfortunes; the philosophies of Heidegger and Jaspers transform each one of us into the interesting interlocutor of a secret and continuous dialogue with nothingness or with divinity; these disciplines, which may be formally admirable, foster the illusion of the self that Vedanta condemns as a capital error. They may play at desperation and anguish, but at bottom they flatter the vanity; in that sense, they are immoral. Shaw's work, on the other hand, leaves an aftertaste of liberation. The taste of the doctrines of Zeno's Porch and the taste of the sagas. (*OI*, 166)

As Borges has himself remarked, all of his books deal, at least in some measure, with time. *Other Inquisitions* is no exception. In addition to the "New Refutation of Time" reprinted in the volume, at least half a dozen other pieces take up various aspects of the subject. The problem of how time can be used in literature provides an especially fertile field for Borges's ruminations. Thus, in "La flor de Coleridge" ("The Flower of Coleridge") he analyzes several techniques for creating fantastic effects through the manipulation of time: Coleridge's use of a flower, which appears first in a dream and then later is present when the dreamer awakes; H. G. Wells's insertion of the "withered flower of the future" in his novel *The Time Machine;* and finally, Henry James's analysis of the possible effects on the present that might result from a trip to the past, as seen in his time-travel story, "The Sense of the Past." One of the most provocative pieces in the collection, "Kafka y sus precursores" ("Kafka and His Precursors"), approaches the question of chronological sequence in an unusual manner. Taken out of context, Borges's statement in the essay that "each writer *creates* his precursors" (*OI*, 108) seems deliberately illogical. Yet what he says is both logical and historically valid, though some may consider it a truism. Borges begins the essay by showing how such dissimilar authors as Zeno, Browning, Leon Bloy, and Kierkegaard have all written certain pages in which a person familiar with Kafka would note a particular idiosyncrasy typical of this modern Czech master. "But if Kafka had never written," Borges explains, "we would not perceive it, it would not exist." Following a thought suggested by T. S. Eliot, Borges sums up his point: "[Every writer's] work modifies our conception of the past, as it will modify the future" (*OI*, 108).

Closely akin to the time theme is Borges's long-standing exploration of the notion of infinitude, evident in this collection in several essays. Even in pieces in which his primary concern is for seemingly unrelated matters, ideas of infinite series, infinite division of time or space into increasingly smaller units, or the opposing—but equally disturbing—notion of a closed, finite universe intrigue him. The fact that in the *Quijote* the hero himself reads the book suggests an infinite series of items contained within other items. This detail in Cervantes' famous work reminds Borges of Josiah Royce's reference to the English monarch who had so huge a map of his kingdom made that on the map itself the map-in-minature again appeared, and on this map, a smaller map, and so on. Another expression of Borges's fascination with infinitude is seen in his interest in problems of a mathematical sort involving "convergences": the best example is again the paradox of Achilles and his race with the tortoise. The famous contest, it may be recalled, was first celebrated by Borges in his collection of 1932, *Discusión*. It reappears, and in perhaps more rigorous form, in an essay of 1939, "Avatares de la tortuga" ("Avatars of the Tortoise"), included in *Other Inquisitions*. Here Borges develops the idea that the "vertiginous" *regressus in infinitum* suggested by the paradox "may be applicable to everything"—to literature, the problem of knowledge, and so on.

If we apply the concept of infinitude to the world, if we say that all things are infinitely divisible, then the symbols we use to describe the world—language—may also be thought of as infinitely divisible. This idea had come up earlier in Borges's essays; in *Other Inquisitions* it appears, perhaps just below the surface, in "El idioma analítico de John Wilkins" ("The Analytical Language of John Wilkins"). In the seventeenth century, Wilkins wrote a treatise on "Philosophical Language" in which he proposed an organized synthetic language. His attempt had all the artificial and arbitrary qualities that any synthetic tongue has. Borges uses the work of this relatively obscure writer as a point of departure for discussing a variety of curious, and often very humorous, attempts of a similar nature. The point of the essay seems to be that language—even naturally evolved language—is no more than an arbitrary system whose "units" may stand for a large segment of what we call reality, or for a minuscule segment. The use of generic linguistic symbols as opposed to specific ones is likewise conventional rather than logically necessary. The essay further suggests the idea, perhaps related to the philosophy of nominalism, that we only delude ourselves if we think of any language as describing all of reality's infinite bits and pieces.

The poetry and essays of Borges's earlier years constitute an important corpus of literary work. Had he never written the superb prose fiction of the forties and fifties, it seems likely that he still would have been considered a writer of some stature. However, after having produced the celebrated work of his middle years—*Ficciones* (1944) and *El Aleph* (*The Aleph,* 1949)—and after achieving recognition beyond the Hispanic world, these formative writings acquired new significance. As we shall see, the literary essays especially have provided a fertile seedbed for cultivation by contemporary critics.

Chapter Two
The Canonical Texts

Borges's present fame rests on a relatively small number of short narratives. While his complete works fill many volumes, and although his essays, poems, and literary musings complement his central achievement, it is this corpus of quintessentially Borgesian texts that have established him as a major voice among Western postmodernists. The bulk of these pieces appear in *Ficciones* (*Ficciones*, 1944) and *El Aleph* (*The Aleph*, 1949, 1952): in terms of their date of composition they represent his work of the mid-thirties through the early fifties. These texts, perhaps only twelve or fifteen in number, have been frequently reedited, widely anthologized, intensively studied, and extensively translated. It is possible that a few of the narratives written in his later years, that is, from the publication of *El hacedor* (*Dreamtigers*, 1960) till his death, will come to be included among this canonical group; but their significance will, I think, always be viewed in relation to his earlier work.

Although he is often considered to be a *cuentista,* a writer of short stories, it is with some trepidation that critics apply this term to Borges. He himself preferred to use the terms *narratives, fictions,* even *artifices* to describe many of these texts; perhaps he sensed that they did not conform to the generally held notion of a short story. Indeed, if one looks for a well-structured plot line complete with some development and a climax, many of Borges's *ficciones* (perhaps the most commonly used descriptive term) will be found lacking. Yet other pieces among the canonical texts are characterized by plots so highly structured that early critics attacked them for being too "geometrical." In short, it is difficult to generalize about Borges's prose fiction, especially if a traditional definition of the genre is used. A number of these pieces could almost be considered fictionalized essays, given the dominance of an idea, a philosophic notion, or a literary concept over narration. Thus in my earlier study of Borges, I used the somewhat awkward term *essayistic fiction* to describe a group of these texts. Finally, the very fact that Borges violated traditional generic boundaries—an acknowledged characteristic of postmodern letters—has contributed to his significance as a major figure of the century.

There are many ways in which Borges's canonical texts might be classified: by date of publication, by theme, or by dominant structural features. A novel scheme might be based on his choice of setting, that is, stories of the mysterious East, Argentine tales, English-Irish pieces, and so forth. The matter of taxonomy is of course quite arbitrary, as Borges himself has wittily pointed out. My own classification of these well-known texts is admittedly idiosyncratic, though I trust not as strange as the zoological taxonomy found in a certain Chinese encyclopedia that Borges once described.

The Reluctant Narrator: "Streetcorner Man" and "The Approach to al-Mu'tasim"

The two prefaces that Borges wrote to his *Historia universal de la infamia* (*A Universal History of Infamy*, 1935) are very revealing. In the first, preceding the original edition, he refers to the book as a collection of "exercises in narrative prose." He modestly goes on to note that "they overly exploit certain tricks: random enumerations, sudden shifts of continuity, and the paring down of a man's whole life into two or three scenes. . . . They are not, they do not try to be, psychological."[1] In the preface to the second edition (1954), he refers to these pieces as "the irresponsible game of a shy young man who dared not write stories and so amused himself by falsifying and distorting (without any aesthetic justification whatever) the tales of others" (*UHI*, 12). The reference to "tales of others" is not without foundation. In a display of literary candor he appends a list of specific sources for the collection: several books on American history, the *Encyclopaedia Britannica,* Mark Twain, etc. Only one text, "El hombre de la esquina rosada" ("Streetcorner Man"), could be considered a genuine and original short story. It is of some significance that Borges first published it under the pseudonym "F. Bustos" in the literary supplement to the Buenos Aires newspaper *Crítica*. Another crucial text for tracing the emergence of Borges's fiction has already been mentioned briefly, "The Approach to al-Mu'tasim," which despite its narrative elements lay buried among the essays of *Historia de la eternidad.*

Critics have offered a number of explanations regarding Borges's early reluctance to write fiction: most of these derive from personal or political factors. Clearly the decade of the thirties was a difficult time for Argentines, especially the country's intellectuals. The first three decades of the century had seen considerable progress toward democracy and material well-being, but with the fall of civilian government in 1930 and the onset of military rule and of what Argentine historians have called "the absurd decade," the mood of the nation became ugly. A reflection of this pessimistic, disruptive atmosphere may be seen in Borges's work, as the critic Emir Rodríguez Monegal has pointed out.[2] It could be argued that the times produced a general insecurity that was hardly propitious for expanding one's horizons or doing new things; and, for Borges, fiction would be a new venture. His essential reserve, his shyness and timidity may well have played a role here: stated simply, he had achieved a modest success as a poet and essayist and was reluctant to strike out into unfamiliar literary territory. Other factors may also lie behind his reluctance to write fiction. We have seen in his literary essays that he had considerable reservations regarding the kind of narratives most appreciated since the nineteenth century—namely the "draggy novel of character," the psychological novel, and similar forms. It is even conceivable that the popularity of this kind of fiction encouraged him to seek innovative forms for his own fictional experiments. In short, during the thirties Borges seemed interested in turning toward fiction but was not quite sure of the path he should follow. Why he finally decided, as the decade closed, to move decisively in this direction is a question that will be answered shortly.

Historia universal de la infamia (*A Universal History of Infamy*, 1935) is a miscellany consisting of eight short sketches or vignettes dealing with famous and not-so-famous ne'er-do-wells; one short story, "Streetcorner Man"; and five very brief glosses of various literary texts. Borges tells us at the outset that "the word 'infamy' in the title is thunderous, but behind the sound and fury there is nothing" (*UHI*, 12). And indeed there is not a great deal here except the charming, and often very funny, manner in which Borges retells the bizarre histories of his antiheroes: Lazarus Morrell, the "atrocious redeemer of slaves," who earned a tidy living by encouraging Negroes to flee their masters and then resold the escapees to other slaveholders; Tom Castro, a subequatorial confidence man who for many years deceived a comfortable widow by claiming to be her long-lost son; the Widow Ching, a completely incongruous cymbal-clashing pirate queen of the China Seas; Monk Eastman, a New York mobster of the turn of the century who, after ten years in Sing Sing Prison and a military career, dies at the hands of an unknown assassin; the coldblooded Bill Harrigan—alias Billy the Kid—whose real and mythical exploits are well known to American readers; one Kotsuké No Suké, a samurai of ancient Japan, whose unforgettable person gives Borges the opportunity to explicate certain details of ancient Nippon's honor code; and finally Ha'kim de Merv, the mysterious and resplendent Veiled Prophet of Islamic lore who is ultimately revealed as a hideously deformed leper. Borges deliberately informs the reader of his factual sources for most of the items—a further indication of his timidity, his desire to appear as a commentator, as a reteller of tales rather than as an original writer. But he was not content simply to recast in his own words what others had written. Rather, Borges changed, modified, and reworked the original materials, expanding a small detail of a source text, omitting or alternating an important event, adding a character here or eliminating a character there. In short, he had begun to write fiction.

"Streetcorner Man" was a rather different text and one that did not depend on other sources unless one counts two very sketchy versions of the story that Borges had written some eight years before. The setting is one that figures in some of his early poetry and one that would haunt him till his death—the picturesque, violent, almost mythic world of Buenos Aires' lower-class neighborhoods of yesteryear. The tale's plot is fairly simple: a *compadre,* or local tough, is challenged by a rival from another district; the first man appears to be a coward and backs off; the rival takes off with his opponent's woman (a sensual beauty, the pride of the local dance hall in which the action takes place); and the narrator, a member of the coward's gang, apparently goes after the rival intruder. The reader is not told exactly what happens, but after a brief absence the narrator returns and a bit later the girl, followed by the dying and bloody abductor, appears. After the latter dies, the unnamed narrator examines his knife and remarks "I turned the blade over, slowly. It was as good as new, innocent-looking, and there wasn't the slightest trace of blood on it" (*UHI,* 98). This frequently anthologized story has enjoyed considerable popularity and was even adapted for the cinema, though in interviews Borges often belittled it.

For students of Borges, "Streetcorner Man" is extremely interesting. The thematic elements—knife fights, the fine line dividing cowardice from valor, the world of the tango, and the general flavor of Buenos Aires street culture—have come to be regarded as hallmarks of Borges's *criollista* modality. Certain narrative techniques typical of his later work also appear in this piece: these include the use of a second-level narrator (the story is told to "Borges" by an anymonous first-person narrator who is one of the chief actors in the plot); the creation of an ambiguous denouement; and the interjection of one or more clues as to what actually happened. Yet other aspects of the story are quite atypical. The language, for example, is at times almost indecipherable to those unfamiliar with *lunfardo,* the street slang of Buenos Aires. Moreover, the coarseness of the language and the direct references to sexual activity at one point in the text seem entirely out of keeping with the voice and tone of Borges's later work. As critics have suggested, the use of a pseudonym and the device of presenting the story as another's tale may stem from Borges's desire to save his proper middle-class family the embarrassment of acknowledging such an audacious author as one of their own.

"The Approach to al-Mu'tasim" is of approximately the same vintage as the *Infamy* vignettes and has some superficial resemblances to them. It too was inspired by other texts, namely, the critical remarks of Phillip Guedalla and Cecil Roberts regarding a book recently published in Bombay by one Mir Bahadur Alí. In his own comments, Borges supplies a fairly detailed plot résumé of the Indian's book and gives considerable information on its publication history, noting that the well-known writer of detective fiction Dorothy Sayers did a prologue for its English edition. At the end of the piece, we are also given, in a long footnote, some erudite material on the author's sources. The unique aspect of this "review," and what makes it different from the *Infamy* pieces, is that it is not a modification of other texts but a cleverly presented hoax: whereas Guedella, Roberts, and Sayers were real people, Mir Bahadur Alí and his fascinating novel never existed. However, the calculated mention of familiar publishers, genuine literary reviews, and real critics give the entire text an air of convincing authenticity. The hoax succeeded so well that Borges later recalled friends who had tried to order copies of "The Approach" from London booksellers. The résumé of the nonexistent novel's plot does, nonetheless, give Borges an opportunity to create his own narrative. Thematically, the tale is of interest because it reveals Borges's early fascination with Middle Eastern culture and letters. Structurally, it is necessarily schematic as it purportedly recounts an entire novel in some five pages. "The Approach" is especially important in that it provided a model for the kind of ventures in literary gamesmanship that would in future charm many a reader while repelling others.

That the thirties were difficult years for the nation and for Borges has already been noted. The close of the decade especially saw some major changes in his personal life that had a considerable bearing on his literary career. His father's declining health and death in 1938 created a situation that led Borges to take a post in a rather drab municipal library. Up to that date young "Georgie," as his Anglophile mother was wont to call him, had not really worked at any remunerative occupation. His activities as a writer and his editorial work for various periodicals absorbed his time but produced very little income. Considering his erudition, it is ironic that he did not have any university training and thus could not lay claim to a truly professional position. This same period also saw a marked deterioration in his vision (a genetic problem that eventually led to almost total blindness), as well as frequent bouts with insomnia. To these problems may be added the fact that he apparently had some unhappy love affairs at the time.[3] Not surprisingly, these years are marked by relatively little creative output: his bibliography for 1937 and 1938 lists only a few very short journalistic essays, a few film reviews, and his one-page book reviews in the popular "family" magazine *El Hogar*.[4] Finally, late in 1938—on Christmas Eve to be exact—he suffered an accident that may have had a profound influence on his literary career. Returning to his apartment late one evening, he slipped on a poorly lit staircase and in falling struck himself sharply on the head.[5] For two weeks he remained hospitalized and in a serious condition. During this period he was plagued by insomnia, fever, and nightmares. While convalescing the fear that his mental powers and writing ability had suffered as a result of the accident constantly disturbed him. Because he had written only a few narratives and thus had no reputation as a creator of fiction, he chose to write some stories just to see if his fears were justified: "I thought I would try my hand at writing an article or poem. But I thought: 'I have written hundreds of articles and poems. If I can't do it, then I'll know at once that I am done for'. . . . So I thought I'd try my hand at something I hadn't done: if I couldn't do it, there would be nothing strange about it."[6]

The immediate result of this experiment was the story "Pierre Menard, autor del Quijote," which appeared in the spring of 1939 in *Sur*. About a year later, "Tlön, Uqbar, Orbis Tertius" appeared, to be followed by the steady stream of "fictions" that brought Borges fame.

There are several slightly different versions of these events, but perhaps not too much importance should be attached to the affair. In retrospect it is difficult to accept the idea that this accident marked a genuine shift in his literary trajectory; after all, with the *Universal History of Infamy*, "Streetcorner Man," and the "Approach to al-Mu'tasim," Borges had already taken, albeit hesitantly, the first steps that would lead to international fame as a writer of fiction.

Dreamfictions: "The South," "The Circular Ruins," and "The Secret Miracle"

That life is or may be a dream is a notion that has found expression in the work of many writers, and in Borges's poems, essays, and fiction, sleep, dreams, and the possibility of dreams occupy an important place. Upon finishing "El Sur" ("The South"), for example, many readers would conclude that the entire text is the recounting of a dream, if not a nightmare. Yet the earlier pages of the text have a rather realistic quality, and the most fascinating aspect of the narrative is that the dream—if there actually is one—

seems to consume reality. Thus the reader wonders at just what point the narrator's awake state ends and his dream begins. "The South" is doubly interesting for those intrigued by the appearance, in thinly disguised form, of autobiographical material: many commentators have pointed out the remarkable parallels between the tale's plot line and the details of Borges's 1938 Christmas accident.

The story itself is deceptively simple. A third-person narrator describes the background of one Johannes Dahlman, a "profoundly" Argentine citizen of German-*criollo* ancestry, who identifies more with the "romantic" heroes of his Argentine forebears than with his staid German ancestors. Though a quiet soul (who incidentally works in a municipal library), he cherishes the old sword of his grandfather, a military hero of the Indian wars on the pampas. Other details, too, reflect the author's own life, not the least of which is that one evening "late in February 1939" (note the minor alteration of the date) he hurts his head by striking something while climbing a dark staircase. As a result of the wound and the septicemia that ensues he is hospitalized for an indefinite period. He is finally released to convalesce at the family ranch somewhere off in the South. Borges describes his protagonist's ride through the city to the railroad terminal, the long train trip into the country, his getting off at a small rural station (an alternate one, not the usual one), and his slight uneasiness on seeing the half-familiar town itself. While waiting for a horse and buggy to be prepared for the final part of the journey, Dahlman decides to eat something in the local general store. It is here that the story builds to its climax. Some rough country types, evidently half drunk, pick a fight with him: one of the group, an especially tough customer, is toying with a knife and eventually challenges Dahlman to a duel. It is at this point, the narrator tells us, that something "unforeseeable" occurs. A mysterious old gaucho, whom Dahlman had noticed earlier, throws a naked dagger at his feet. It may be noted in passing that this is one of many examples in Borges's work of how weapons, especially knives, appear suddenly and are infused with almost magical, autonomous powers. "It was as if the South had resolved that Dahlman should accept the duel. Dahlman bent over to pick up the dagger, and felt two things. The first, that this almost instinctive act bound him to fight. The second, that the weapon, in his torpid hand, was no defense at all, but would merely serve to justify his murder. . . . *They would not have allowed such things to happen to me in the sanatarium,* he thought."[7] Though he is unskilled in knife fighting and feels certain he will die, at the every end of the story Dahlman accepts his destiny with the thought that when on that distant night in the sanatorium they stuck him with a needle, "that to die in a knife fight, under the open sky . . . would have been a liberation, a joy, and a festive occasion. . . . He felt that if he had been able to choose, then, or to dream his death, this would have been the death, he would have chosen or dreamt" (PA, 23).

This ambivalent conclusion suggests, but does not clearly establish, that the bulk of the tale has been simply a dream. The possibility that virtually everything since "a masked man" injected Dahlman in the hospital has existed only in the sick man's delirious imagination is very strong. A number of other details in the text point toward this interpretation: the fact that Dahlman thinks that the owner of the general store looks like one of the hospital staff; the thought that events like these "would not have been allowed . . . in the sanitarium." Yet the brief mention earlier in the story that Dahlman dozes on and off during the train trip and especially the narrator's description of the protagonist's reflections while traveling invite us to conjecture that the dream begins on the train: "Tomorrow I'll wake up at the ranch, he thought, and it was as if he were two men at a time: the man who traveled through the autumn day and across the geography of the fatherland, and the other one, locked up in a sanitarium" (PA, 19). An even earlier starting point for the "dreamt" portion of the text is obliquely suggested by Borges's underscoring the significance of Dahlman's crossing Rivadavia Street on his way to the railroad station: "Every Argentine knows that the South begins on the other side of Rivadavia . . . that whoever crosses this street enters a more ancient and sterner world" (PA, 18). In other words, he crosses over from the real world to a mythic—or dreamlike—realm. These speculations inevitably lead back to the question of deciding whether or not the tale, or a portion of it, is in fact a dream. But why should we concern ourselves with this problem? After all, are not all fictions by definition simply creations of the imagination which may thus be considered a kind of literary dream? And if this is so, a "dream" inserted into any fictional piece becomes nothing more than a dream within a dream.

"Las ruinas circulares" ("The Circular Ruins"), a tale that is structured around a very Borgesian extension of the dream concept, is deservedly one of the most anthologized pieces in Ficciones. Unlike several of the other texts in the collection, it is a genuine story complete with an element of suspense and a kind of surprise ending. The opening lines set a mood of mystery well calculated to capture the reader's attention: "No one saw him disembark in the unanimous night, no one saw the bamboo canoe sinking into the sacred mud, but within a few days no one was unaware that the silent man came from the South and that his home was one of the infinite villages upstream on the violent side of the mountain, where the Zend tongue is not contaminated with Greek."[8] The mysterious traveler, described as "the gray man," kisses the mud, ascends the river bank, without pushing aside the brambles that "dilacerated" his flesh, and lies exhausted and asleep. A significant detail that Borges notes parenthetically is that he "probably did not feel" the thorns as he passed through them.

The spot where the stranger lies asleep is a "Circular enclosure crowned by a stone horse or tiger, which once was the color of fire and now was that of ashes. This circle was a temple, long ago devoured by fire" (*L,* 45). Upon awakening, Borges tells us, the man knows that this is the precise place required to carry out his "purpose," the exact nature of which is clarified shortly: "The purpose which guided him was not impossible, though it was supernatural. He wanted to dream a man: he wanted to dream him with minute integrity and insert him into reality" (*L,* 46). What follows is the detailed description of how the protagonist goes about his task.

At first he attempts to dream a "class" of disciples—a large group from whom he might select, or "redeem," a single individual to "insert" into reality. After a number of unsuccessful efforts he decides that he must concentrate intensely on just one of the group. But his attempt fails; he suffers insomnia; he becomes infuriated and frustrated. Finally he comes to the conclusion that he must abandon his original method completely, He spends a month recuperating his powers before again undertaking his arduous task. He gives up trying to dream and, as a result, he finds he sleeps more easily and that once again he is able to dream. Ready to begin his project anew, "he purified himself in the waters of the river, worshiped the planetary gods, uttered the permitted syllables of a powerful name and slept" (*L,* 47). At this point he dreams of a beating heart. He now understands how he can accomplish his objective. As a sculptor carefully chisels a masterpiece, the "gray man" slowly fashions his creation. Starting with the internal organs he painstakingly dreams the arteries, the skeleton, and the eyelids. "The innumerable hair was perhaps the most difficult task," he tells us. After a year, the dream child is physically complete. Finally, "In the dreamer's dream, the dreamed one awoke" (*L,* 48).

The protagonist devotes some two years to instructing his child in the mysteries of the universe and in the enigmatic details of the "fire cult." The son is now ready to leave: his father kisses him and sends him off to another temple far downstream where, presumably, he would fulfill his duties as a priest of his cult. However, before he departs, his father instills in him the "complete oblivion of his years of apprenticeship" (*L,* 49). His purpose in doing this, as Borges notes parenthetically, is to make him think that he is a man, not a phantom. At any rate, the son leaves, and the parent, saddened by his departure, is left to meditate. His thoughts continue to be troubled by the fear that his son might in some way learn that his existence was merely illusory, and he muses, "Not to be a man, to be the projection of another man's dream, what a feeling of humiliation, of vertigo!" (*L,* 50).

At this point in the story, smoke appears in the distance, then the flight of animals. Finally the "gray man" realizes that a ring of fire is closing in on him. At first he thinks of trying to escape into the river; but he is old and tired, and he knows that inevitable death is coming to "absolve him of his labors." The flames come closer and begin to engulf him. But he feels neither heat nor combustion. The last two lines of the tale reveal what the astute reader has perhaps already guessed: "With relief, with humiliation, with terror, he understood that he too was a mere appearance, dreamt by another" (*L,* 50).

A wealth of Borgesian ideas underlies the story: the Berkeleyan notion of existence as a function of perception, carried to the extreme of "dreaming" objects into the real world, is blended with Gnostic cosmology and the idea of a creator-behind-the-creator. The suggestion of an infinite regression also is evident: the "gray man" dreams a son who quite naturally will dream another son, and so on. Yet these ideas lie just below the surface. Except for a brief mention of the Gnostics and the ancient cult of fire, the story flows smoothly along in the best tradition of genuine fantastic fiction. And, as in detective stories, the most minute details become significant once we know the story's final outcome. For example, the color *gray,* which Borges first uses to describe his protagonist, clearly suggests his shadowy existence; the early mention of *another* distant temple may well be a reference to the protagonist's own origins; and his careful plan to erase all memory of his son's creation may be viewed as an echo of what had been done to him. To sum up, the balancing of all these elements—the underlying philosophic concepts, the mood and language of genuine fantasy, and the structure of a detective story—have produced one of Borges's most impressive compositions. Moreover, for the student of narratology the story raises an interesting question. Note again the very first lines, "no one" sees the protagonist embark: in other words, we have what may be called an "impossible narrator," unless one imagines a divinely omniscient god-narrator, a thought that perhaps adds to the tale's total impact.

Borges's ever-present obsession with time is closely related to his interest in dreams. We know from our own experience and from what psychologists tell us that the duration of dreams bears little relationship to the time perceived by the dreamer. Another aspect of the question arises from the folkloric tradition of considering dreams as capable of carrying us forward in time, as being prophetic. Finally, the imagination, the creative process may be viewed as a kind of dreaming in a special state. These three notions come together very effectively in "El milagro secreto" ("The Secret Miracle"), our last example of what I have called dreamfictions. The story is set in Prague during World War II. Jaromir Hladík, a scholar and author of works dealing with Jewish philosophy, dreams of a long chess game in which the players were entire families and the stakes "enormous." Hladík's confused dream is abruptly ended at dawn, as he hears the rumble of German armor entering the city. He soon gets into difficulties with the Nazis; Hladík's is eventually arrested and sentenced to death, though his crimes are nothing more than his Jewish blood and the signing of a protest against the German occupation. Having presented these basic facts, Borges describes in some detail Hladík's literary interests; not only is he a writer of scholarly works, but he is a poet and dramatist as well. His current project, a drama in verse that he had hoped would be his masterpiece, was, at the time of his arrest, only partially completed, though its main features were all sketched out in his mind.

While awaiting execution he fearfully imagines the circumstances of his forthcoming death: "Before the day set . . . he died hundreds of deaths in courtyards whose forms and angles strained geometrical possibilities. . . . He faced these imaginary executions with real terror (perhaps with real bravery); each simulacrum lasted only a few seconds" (*L,* 89). To escape from these thoughts he desperately seeks surcease in sleep. As 29 March, the day of execution, approaches, he reasons, "I am now in the night of the twenty-second; while this night lasts . . . I am invulnerable, immortal" (*L,* 90). He also becomes increasingly concerned about his yet uncompleted drama, *The Enemies.* Borges sets forth the main lines of this mysterious tragicomedy, the most interesting feature of which is its circularity: in Hladík's rough plot sketch the drama begins in the evening as the clock strikes seven, ends as the same hour is struck, and concludes with an actor repeating the same lines that he had spoken at the play's beginning. But while Hladík had formulated this plot he had only completed the first act. The very night before he is to face the firing squad, just a few minutes before dropping off to sleep, Hladík asks God to grant him a year to complete the entire drama. He falls into a deep sleep but as dawn approaches, Borges tells us, Hladík has yet another confused dream in which he searches for God—in a library—and is finally rewarded by hearing a voice tell him, "The time of your labor has been granted" (*L,* 92). He wakes and at precisely 8:44 he is taken out to the barracks wall. His execution is scheduled for nine o'clock sharp.

Borges etches the scene in fine detail: "Someone pointed out that the wall was going to be stained with blood; the victim was ordered to step forward a few paces. Incongruously, this reminded Hladík of the fumbling preparations of photographers" (*L,* 93). Note this last detail: a very ordinary comparison—one within the experience of any reader—drives home the horror of the scene with chilling fidelity. The guns converge on Hladík, and the sergeant raises his arm to signal the squad to fire, but at this instant Hladík sees the world before him "freeze." The wind stops; the soldiers are motionless; a bee in the courtyard casts "an unchanging shadow." Hladík himself is paralyzed: only his mind is active. He feels no fatigue and even falls asleep. Upon awakening, the scene before him remains frozen exactly as it was. After a while he realizes that God has granted his request. Overcome with gratitude, he begins his year's work—the composition of the remaining portions of his drama. Using only his memory, he lovingly and meticulously revises and reworks the last two acts of his masterpiece. Finally, "He had only the problem of a single phrase. He found it . . . He opened his mouth in a maddened cry, moved his face, dropped under the quadruple blast" (*L,* 94). In the last sentence Borges notes that "Jaromir Hladík died on March 29, at 9:02 a.m."

"The Secret Miracle" is, like "The South" and "The Circular Ruins," a well-structured tale in which the line between explicable reality and the unreal is deliberately indeterminate, or "blurred."[9] Though quite different in each story, a device that produces this blurred quality or ambiguity is some form of dream or mental activity akin to dreaming.

The Ambivalent Hero: "The Shape of the Sword," "The Garden of the Forking Paths," and "The Life of Tadeo Isidoro Cruz"

In a substantial number of Borges's stories the protagonist has what may facetiously be called a serious identity problem. In these pieces the central character may have a double existence, he may be defined entirely by his relationship to a counterpart character, or he may be hidden behind the narrator's voice. We have already seen some heroes of this type: Dahlman is both a convalescing librarian and a knife fighter facing death on the pampa; the "gray man" of the "Circular Ruins" is the product of another's dream; and even Hladík, although he is a real person and has no double, has a somewhat ambiguous personality as seen when he is described as facing the firing squad "with real terror" *or* "perhaps with real bravery." The mystical idea that all men are one, and its corollary that under certain circumstances the villain may be a hero, or vice versa, appears frequently in Borges's work. Even his interest in the Gnostic inversion of good and evil—the Judas figure, for example—may be related to his conviction that only the finest of lines divides the world's saints and heroes from its most despised villains. Borges's fascination with the notion of ambivalence in personality may well be a reflection of his own psyche. Though the temptation to psychoanalyze is great, it should be resisted: suffice it to say that despite his retiring manner, Borges had always been intrigued by bandits—*compadritos*—and by men of action and violence. But aside from the theme's psychological or philosophical ramifications, it certainly provides the basis for a good story.

"A spiteful scar crossed his face: an ash-colored and nearly perfect arc that creased his temple at one tip and his cheek at the other. His real name is of no importance" (*L,* 67). With this vigorous description Borges introduces the protagonist of "La forma de la espada" ("The Shape of the Sword"). We learn that "the Englishman," as his Latin American neighbors call him, is in fact a hard-drinking, cruel, taciturn Irishman who has immigrated to the border country of southern Brazil and northern Argentina. How he earns his living is uncertain: some say he's a smuggler, others a sugar grower. One evening, a sudden rise in a river forces the narrator, who incidentally is revealed as 'Borges' at the tale's end, to spend an evening with this colorful expatriate. The two strike up an after-dinner conversation in the course of which "the Englishman" relates his adventures as a rebel in the Irish independence movement.

The central figure in his tale is John Vincent Moon, another young rebel whom he describes as "slender and flaccid at the same time; he gave the impression of being invertebrate." As the tale develops, it becomes clear that Moon was, in sharp contrast to the narrator, a coward. Moon flees the thick of battle, makes much of a superficial wound, and is given to nervous sobbing when the going gets rough. The fortunes of the revolution meanwhile take a turn for the worse, and the city the Irish rebels are trying to hold falls to the British. One afternoon, the narrator discovers Moon talking on the telephone—obviously to the enemy, and obviously informing on the Irish. Infuriated, he pursues the traitor, seizes him, and then, using an old curved cutlass from the wall of the house in which they are staying, carves into Moon's face "a half-moon of blood." As "the Englishman" relates these events his hands begin shaking. When the narrator inquires as to the ultimate fate of the traitor, he is told that "He collected his Judas money and fled to Brazil" (*L,* 71). At this point the "Englishman" cannot continue; when urged to go on, he blurts out the truth: "Don't you see that I carry written on my face the mark of my infamy? I have told you the story thus so that you would hear me to the end. . . . I am Vincent Moon. Now despise me" (*L*, 71).

Both the framing device and the "switch" at the end are old techniques in the art of fiction. Certainly they are familiar to readers of detective tales and other popular genres. As in the best examples of this kind of work, there is a certain pleasure in reexamining the story to find the thinly veiled clues that hint at the final outcome. Such clues abound in Borges's tale. The very first line mentions the "*spiteful* scar" on the "Englishman's" face; before the narrator begins his story he tells Borges that he's not English but Irish, at which point he is described as "stopping short, as if he had revealed a secret" (*L*, 68), and at the start of his narration, he mentions that many of his comrades were by now dead, including "the most worthy, who died in the courtyard of a barracks" (*L*, 68). Like the other clues, this last one is obviously a reference to the rebel leader whom Moon denounced to the British; but like all good clues, they only become obvious after the cat is let out of the bag. As the "Englishman" reveals more of his story, the clues become more frequent and perhaps more obvious: the fact that Moon, though young and new to the group, was constantly inquiring into the plans of the rebel unit is a case in point. And just before the denouement the "Englishman" comes very close to revealing his true identity when he describes Moon: "This frightened man mortified me, as if I were the coward, not Vincent Moon" (*L*, 70). His philosophic musings following this statement shed further light on some of Borges's own notions regarding individuality: "Whatever one man does, it is as if all men did it. For that reason it is not unfair that one disobedience in a garden should contaminate all humanity; for that reason it is not unjust that the crucifixion of a single Jew should be sufficient to save it. Perhaps Schopenhauer was right: I am all other men; any man is all men, Shakespeare is in some manner the miserable John Vincent Moon" (*L*, 70).

A number of other well known *ficciones* are structured in a somewhat similar manner. "El tema del traidor y el héroe" ("Theme of the Traitor and the Hero") is one, as is the complex and very bookish "El inmortal" ("The Immortal"). Unfortunately, space does not permit a discussion of these tales here.[10]

On first reading, many would consider "El jardín de senderos que se bifurcan" ("The Garden of the Forking Paths") to be simply a spy or detective story, albeit with an unusual twist at the end. Indeed, Borges himself characterizes it as such in the charmingly innocent prologue to the collection in which it first appeared. Yet this deceptively straightforward tale has intrigued many a critic and provides a wealth of material illustrative of

Borges's narrative techniques, not the least of which is his creation of ambivalent characters.

The story itself is related in the form of a dictated statement by a Dr. Yu Tsun whom we learn, as the tale unfolds, is in England and is awaiting execution as a condemned agent for the Germans during World War I. The plot, leaving aside the considerable rich internal detail, is quite simple. Yu Tsun is a Chinese professor of English who had taught at a German school in Tsing Tao. For motives that are not entirely clear, though pride in his race seems to be one, he becomes an agent for the Germans. His specific objective in this story is to communicate to Berlin the exact name of the town in which the British were massing their artillery preparatory to a major offensive. However, the protagonist's immediate superior, one Viktor Runeberg,[11] has been captured, and hence Yu knows that his normal lines of communication to Berlin no longer exist, that the British agents are surely aware of his own identity as a spy, and that even now they are hot on his trail. Convinced that escape is impossible, he is nonetheless determined to communicate his information to Berlin. In the space of ten minutes he devises a plan, the nature of which is only revealed at the story's end. He studies the telephone directory in his room and enigmatically observes that it "listed the name of the only person capable of transmitting the message; he lived in the suburb of Fenton, less than a half hour's ride away" (L, 47). Yu quickly takes the train for the suburb, and even as it leaves the station he sees the British agent Madden running desperately down the platform after him. Arriving in the country, he hurries to the home of a Mr. Stephen Albert, who, by a strange coincidence, happens to be a former missionary to China and an ardent sinologist. Albert, who apparently mistakes his visitor for an acquaintance in the Chinese consular service, invites Yu in. The two soon become engaged in a discussion of the work of one Ts'ui Pên, an ancient Chinese astrologer and writer who was, coincidentally, an ancestor of the protagonist. Because Yu calculates that it will be an hour before his pursuers can overtake him, he chats amiably with Albert about the ancient sage and the literary labyrinth he had composed—an unusual book, entitled *The Garden of the Forking Paths* (*El jardín de senderos que se bifurcan*). But Yu's brief hour hurries by, and finally he is forced to perform the act that had brought him to this particular place. When his host's back is turned, Yu Tsun carefully withdraws his revolver and kills Stephen Albert. At this moment the British agent Madden breaks in and arrests Yu. In the last paragraph of the story we learn that the newspaper reports of the murder of one Stephen Albert by a certain Yu Tsun reach Berlin, and that from them the chief German

intelligence officer easily extracts a vital bit of information, namely, that
the British were massing artillery, preparatory to an offensive, at the
French town of Albert. At the tale's conclusion Yu Tsun explains: "The
chief had deciphered this mystery. He knew my problem was to indicate
(through the uproar of the war) the city called Albert, and that I had
found no other means to do so than to kill a man of that name. He does
not know (no one can know) my innumerable contribution and weariness"
(*L*, 29).

As noted, critics have found in this text a variety of effective Borgesian
narrative techniques: the prefiguring of the outcome by carefully embedded
details, the tale-within-a-tale device, as seen in Albert's literary detective
work to determine the nature of the original "Garden of the Forking Paths,"
and the insertion (deliberate?) of "loose ends," or unresolved details that in a
sense "open" the text to the possibility of additional untold stories.[12] But
"The Garden" is especially interesting as an example of Borges's penchant
for developing ambivalent protagonists. In the first place, Yu Tsun gains
Albert's confidence through his host's apparently mistaking him for someone else, namely, "Hsi P'eng," a Chinese consul in Britain. Yu Tsun never
corrects his host's misconception; thus one may assume that the entire plot
from this point on is driven by mistaken identity. Even if we overlook this
detail, it can be argued that the almost mathematically balanced characteri-
zations of Yu Tsun and Stephen Albert produce a situation of inverted doubles in which the two are in effect "identical and opposite."[13] But this
analogous relationship is only part of Borges's threat to what one critic has
called "the absolute autonomy of the self":

The very repetition of the act of variation, involving a chain of quotations, makes
the story a perfect example of what Jakobson calls "speech within speech" and di-
vorces the various characters from their own discourse. In addition to the real author's speech to the real reader, crystallized in that of the implied author to the
implied reader, the whole story is the speech of an extradiegetic–heterodiegetic narrator who, in a footnote, calls himself "editor". . . . First as the editor quotes T'sun,
so T'sun, an extradiegetic-homodiegetic narrator, quotes Albert who in turn quotes
T'sui Pen. . . . Quotation, then, is a dominant narrative mode in this story, and
quotation is the appropriation by one person of the speech of another. Since a person is to a large extent constituted by his discourse, such an appropriation implies,
at least partly, an interpenetration of personalities. Thus both repetition through
analogy and repetition through quotation threaten the absolute autonomy of the
self.[14]

A different sort of loss of autonomy shapes the central character of "Biografía de Tadeo Isidoro Cruz" ("The Life of Tadeo Isidoro Cruz"). In this case the ambivalent nature of the hero depends to a great extent on the reader's familiarity with the background material on which the story is based. The innocent reader, who would almost have to be a non-Argentine, finds the text to be an apparently historical account of one Tadeo Isidoro Cruz, an obscure gaucho born out of wedlock during Argentina's civil wars of the early nineteenth century. Borges tells us how he grew up in total ignorance of civilization, how he got into a knife fight, killed a man, was thrown into the army as a punishment, and was wounded in combat with the Indians. The author makes no claims to completeness or accuracy in his recounting of Cruz's life; however, he does carefully inform us that "Of the many days and nights that make up his life, only a single night concerns me; as to the rest, I shall tell only what is necessary to that night's full understanding."[15] He also notes, in a hint that Argentines and students of its literature might pick up, that "The episode belongs to a famous poem—that is to say, to a poem which has come to mean 'all things to all men'" (*AOS*, 82). At any rate, Borges completes "the dim and hardy story" of his protagonist's life to that decisive point "during the last days of the month of June 1870" when Cruz, now a sergeant, is sent out with a squad of men to capture a notorious outlaw and deserter from the army.

On the night of 12 July, we are told, he finds his quarry, who refuses to surrender, forcing Cruz and his men to fight. Borges slyly observes, "An obvious reason keeps me from describing the fight that followed. Let me simply point out that the deserter badly wounded or killed several of Cruz's men" (*AOS*, 84). He goes on to analyze his protagonist's transformation at this point in the tale: "He understood that one destiny is no better than another, but that every man must obey what is within him. . . . He understood that his real destiny was a lone wolf, not a gregarious dog. He understood that the other man was himself. . . . Cruz threw down his kepi, called out that he would not be a party to the crime of killing a brave man, and began fighting against his own soldiers, shoulder to shoulder with Martín Fierro, the deserter" (*AOS*, 85).

There are a number of reasons why the foregoing well illustrates the Borgesian penchant for ambiguity and for undermining the identity of his characters. In the first place, the piece—for those familiar with its historical and literary allusions—presents a strange situation indeed: the "intersection" of a completely fictional creation from a literary work ("Sargento Cruz" appears in José Hernández's 1871 epic poem of the gaucho, *Martín Fierro*) with another seemingly historical person to whom Borges gives a first name and enough biographical detail to make him quite believable. Second, the specific incident in the *Martín Fierro* that Borges focuses on itself provides an excellent example of ambivalence and change of identity. Sergeant Cruz (as his very name implies) "crosses over" from the world of law and order to join Fierro the outlaw; moreover, his life and to an extent his attitudes form a set of doubles and counterparts to those of Fierro so that "the other man was himself," to use Borges's exact words. Even the motivation for Cruz's decision is fraught with ambiguity: since his men were being decimated by Fierro, there is a real question as to why he made his dramatic move. Was Cruz a genuine hero who could not witness the sight of the outnumbered Fierro fighting off the soldiers, or was he a cowardly opportunist who, sensing that the tide of battle was going against him, decided to save his skin by joining the outlaw? Of course these questions are not dealt with in Borges's text, but for the knowledgeable reader they are inherent in the story. Thus, by a masterful stroke of intertextual appropriation, Borges takes full advantage of the underlying ambivalence in another text, namely, Hernández's celebrated epic poem of the nineteenth century.

Games of the Mind: "Funes the Memorious," "The Library of Babel," "The Lottery in Babylon," and "Tlön, Uqbar, Orbis Tertius"

The texts to be examined next belong to a group of almost unclassifiable pieces that derive from mathematical notions or philosophical ideas. Although they have definite narrative elements, they have a stronger expository thrust and thus can almost be thought of as "essayistic fiction." They are highly imaginative, very cerebral, and often spiced with details dear to bibliophiles.

A few words will suffice to describe one of the least complex of these texts, "Funes el memorioso" ("Funes the Memorious"), a piece that recalls Borges's long-standing interest in problems of language and in the nature of memory. The central character, Ireneo Funes, is a lad of the Uruguayan pampas who, after a serious accident, becomes aware of the fact that he has a complete and photographic memory. Bits and pieces of his strange existence are described: how he calmly and effortlessly memorized the entire Latin text of Pliny's *Natural History;* how the complete causal train of events that stand behind any perceived object was known to him; how he attempted to organize and codify the vast storehouse of his memory; and how he suffered insomnia as a result of the myriads of precise impressions that crowded his mind. Borges uses the piece to digress on such arcane themes as the possibility of establishing an "infinite vocabulary" corresponding to the natural series of numbers, and Locke's project of devising "an impossible language in which each individual thing, each stone, each bird, and each branch, would have its own name" (*L*, 65). These themes are closely related to Borges' interest in nominalism and to his ideas on language, as expressed in such essays as "Indagación de la palabra" (Inquiry into words) and "The Analytical language of John Wilkins." Though there is a note of horror in Funes's unusual gift—or curse—Borges emphasizes the intellectual content of the piece rather than the protagonist's personal destiny. Thus, a single line describes the end of Funes's shadowy existence: "Ireneo Funes died in 1889, of congestion of the lungs" (*L*, 66). Of greater importance, perhaps, is Borges's comment on the relationship of memory and forgetting to the nature of understanding: "With no effort he had learned English, French, Portuguese and Latin. I suspect, however, that he was not very capable of thought. To think is to forget differences, generalize, make abstractions. In the teeming world of Funes, there were only details, almost immediate in their presence" (*L*, 66).

From his earliest years as a writer Borges was fascinated by logical paradoxes, by numerology, and (though he seldom used the technical terms) by such concepts as subsets, probability, permutations, and combinations. In two well-known texts, "La biblioteca de Babel" ("The Library of Babel") and "La lotería in Babilonia" ("The Lottery in Babylon"), mathematical notions figure prominently. These two pieces also illustrate Borges's cultivation of a single object or institution—a book, a sphere, a library, or even a text—that provides the key to the universe: the "emblem" or "open sesame" revealing a hidden order or secret plan of the cosmos.

"The universe (which others call the Library) is composed of an indefinite and perhaps infinite number of hexagonal galleries" (*L*, 51), Borges tells us in the opening lines of "The Library of Babel." The parenthesis immediately informs us that the particular symbol or emblem of reality to be employed in the piece is the Book, or, to be more accurate, a collection of books, the Library. The various ways in which the narrator attempts to render the physical aspect of the Library echoes a number of other Borgesian pieces: its form is geometric, an indefinite number of hexagonal galleries placed one atop the other with a central shaft or air space throughout, but its extent is infinite. Like a great circular book, "The Library is a sphere whose exact center is any one of its hexagons and whose circumference is inaccessible" (*L*, 52).

In the main portion of the piece the nameless narrator explains the principal "axioms" on which the Library is organized. First of all, the Library exists eternally; second, there are twenty-five orthographical symbols which all the Library's books are based (twenty-two letters, comma, period, and space). He explains that each book consists of 410 pages; each page of forty lines; and each line of approximately eighty letters. In brief, the Library is the product of all the possible permutations and combinations of the twenty-five symbols arranged within the format just described. While the number of different volumes would necessarily be incredibly huge, given these specific limitations, it would not be infinite. Yet the structure of the Library itself, as we just saw, is described in terms clearly suggesting infinitude. Borges's final resolution of the problem posed by the situation—a finite number of items filling an infinite space—is perfectly logical: "*The Library is unlimited and cyclical.* If an eternal traveler were to cross it in any direction, after centuries he would see that the same volumes were repeated in the same disorder (which, thus repeated, would be an order: the Order)" (*L,* 58). If we recall that the Library is equated with the universe, we can see a number of typically Borgesian ideas reflected in this symbolism. If the "books" are thought of as people or events, notions of cyclical historicism and the idea that there is nothing really new under the sun immediately come to mind.

But "The Library of Babel" is more than an intellectual exercise in permutation and combination. The "Men of the Library," mysterious and tragic figures who roam the endless galleries in search of general truth or specific answers to troublesome questions, are seldom rewarded for their labors. More often than not they find only hopelessly garbled volumes that often contain only one line of tantalizingly clear language. All possible languages, and combinations of language, are found in the *almost* infinite number of volumes. For example, one "chief of an upper hexagon" discovers, after much study, that a certain volume is written in "a Samoyedic Lithuanian dialect of Guarani, with classical Arabian inflections" (*L,* 54). There are virtually no conceivable orthographic combinations not found in the Library. The narrator tells how, in his own hexagon, may be found such intriguing titles as *The Combed Thunderclap, The Plaster Cramp,* or, even better, *Axaxaxas mlö.*[16] Borges notes that "these phrases at first glance incoherent, can no doubt be justified in a cryptographical or allegorical manner" (*L,* 57). Even more dizzying is the thought that somewhere in the Library the *key* to such cryptic works must exist! Some of the lonely librarians (their number, we are told, seems to be steadily diminishing) search for books of prophecy; others for "vindications," that is, books that "justify" the existence of a particular individual; still others seek among endless galleries of "false" catalogues the "catalogue of catalogues."

Lurking just below the surface of all this description is a rich and provocative Borgesian allegory of universal history, of man's search for truth, of his ephemeral moments of triumph, of the folly of his sectarian conflicts, and most of all, of the futility of his attempts to solve riddles of an eternal or absolute nature. Borges's description of the "official searchers" as they return from their labors brings out this mood very effectively: "they always arrive extremely tired from their journeys; they speak of a broken stairway which almost killed them . . . sometimes they pick up the nearest volume and leaf through it, looking for infamous words. Obviously, no one expects to discover anything" (*L*, 55). Although "The Library of Babel" has no plotted story, the dramatic allegorical rendering of man's quest sets it apart from Borges's essays and his essayistic fiction.

"The Lottery in Babylon" bears some resemblance to the tale just discussed. "Babylon," like the word "library," is an emblem or rubric that stands for the universe. In this story, however, Borges emphasizes a slightly different aspect of man's puny efforts to make sense out of an essentially unfathomable world. The broad metaphor of "the lottery," as Borges develops it, deals with the notion that there is a clearly distinguishable difference between chance happenings and ordered events. People quite naturally believe—at least before they read "La lotería en Babilonia"— that this is so. After all, theologies have been constructed about the crucial concepts of free will versus determinism, and philosophical systems have used the notions of contingency and necessity as basic building blocks. The nameless narrator of "The Lottery," however, comes from a place where these important distinctions are blurred, a "dizzy land where the lottery is the basis of reality" (*L*, 30).

The story of how the lottery developed from an elementary pastime to become the dominant feature of the world provides the basic material for this piece. The narrator explains how at first the lower classes of Babylon would buy "chances" for a few pennies in the hopes of winning a small prize; barbers were the traditional lottery vendors, and drawings were uncomplicated affairs held in the open. Gradually, to encourage interest, a new element was added. Some of those who held "unlucky" numbers not only lost their original investment but also had to pay small fines. If these unfortunate players refused to pay these trifling amounts, the "Company" (for the lottery was now institutionalized and controlled by a mysterious organization) might sue them and even put them in jail. After a while, the losers were not fined at all, but simply incarcerated for a fixed number of days. In

this manner the lottery's original monetary basis was altered so that soon
both winners and losers received their prizes or punishments in nonmone-
tary form. In time the "Company" succeeded in making the operation of the
lottery secret, free, and obligatory for all. Further refinements were soon
added: a loser's ultimate fate might be altered by a "bifurcation," or lottery-
within-the-lottery. The moment before his execution he might be forced to
draw nine numbers, one of which could mitigate this extreme penalty, another of which might grant him a full pardon, while yet another might enti-
tle him to a great prize. In like manner, a winner might find a treasure
snatched from his grasp at the last moment: "In reality the *number of drawings is infinite*. No decision is final, all branch into others" (*L*, 34). In characteristic Borgesian fashion, the central idea of the all-pervading lottery is
unrelentingly carried to its logical conclusion. "Babylon" becomes so thoroughly infused with chance that the very meaning of the word is lost. Behind all these happenings is the enigmatic "Company" whose orders,
incidentally, *may* not be genuine, but rather the work of "impostors." In
such a world who can distinguish what is counterfeit from what is genuine?
In the last paragraph of the piece the narrator concludes, "The Company's
silent operations, comparable to God's, give rise to all sorts of conjectures
. . . that the Company has not existed for centuries and that the sacred disorder of our lives is purely hereditary, traditional . . . that the Company is
omnipotent, but that it only has influence in tiny things. . . . Another, in
the words of masked heresiarchs, *that it has never existed and will not exist*.
Another, no less vile, reasons that it is indifferent to affirm or deny the reality of the shadowy corporation, because Babylon is nothing else than an infinite game of chance" (*L*, 35).

   Like a number of other Borgesian texts, "The Lottery" is developed from
the relentless and vertiginous expansion of a relatively simple idea into
nightmarish proportions. Certain formal features of the piece also contrib-
ute to this effect. For example, recent critics, sensitive to the subtleties of
narrative art, have noted that lurking behind Borges's text we have a very
human and very harried narrator, whose only personal remark in the midst
of the account, "I don't have much time left; they tell us the ship is about to
weigh anchor" (*L*, 33), opens up the text to the possibility of another, untold, but very intriguing tale.

   From its enigmatic title to the pathos of its final paragraphs, few texts of
Borges have elicited more critical attention or have confounded more readers
than "Tlön, Uqbar, Orbis Tertius." As one of his longer pieces, it provides
ample opportunity for Borges to explore and interrelate several favorite
themes: Berkeleyian idealism, "the book" or collection of books as an em-

blem of the universe, and the arbitrary nature of language. Moreover, "Tlön," as James Irby has astutely observed, "perhaps more fully than any other of his fictions . . . declares their basic principles, characteristically making of that declaration a fictionalized essay, a creation which studies itself."[17] Its essayistic or philosophical content notwithstanding, "Tlön" has considerable narrative structure, a genuine plot that only becomes obvious when the final section is read. The text is further enriched by Borges's oblique comments regarding the contemporary world, the perils of the future, and his own retreat into the protective cover of literary activity.

The piece consists of three main divisions: the "discovery" and description of Uqbar, an apocryphal land vaguely suggestive of somewhere in the Middle East; the essay on the strange planet of Tlön, where idealism and psychological association dominate; and finally, the crucial "1947 Postscript," which despite its apparent date was an integral part of the original 1940 text. Borges, as the identified narrator, begins the first section in a chatty, familiar tone by telling how one evening his very real friend Bioy Casares happened to make a casual reference to a religious writer of Uqbar. When Borges confessed that he was unfamiliar with both the writer and the land of Uqbar, Bioy replied that his information came from the *Anglo-American Cyclopedia,* a set of which just happens to be in the house Borges had recently rented. However, on examining the encyclopedia (a "delinquent pirating" of the tenth edition of the *Britannica,* Borges notes parenthetically), they find no article on Uqbar. Dismayed and confused, they agree that it must exist somewhere in either the Near or Middle East. The next day Bioy calls Borges to inform him that he has located a copy of the encyclopedia, which does indeed contain the piece on Uqbar. On careful examination of the particular volume they find that Borges's copy contains only 917 pages, whereas Bioy's had 921, the four extra pages being those describing Uqbar. The article itself, characterized by "rigorous prose" beneath which was "a fundamental vagueness," gave no concrete statement regarding Uqbar's exact location. Further checking, in such standard works as Perthe's atlas and Ritter's geography, reveals nothing whatever about this mysterious land.

The riddle of Uqbar is left unsolved, and the events described in the second section take place two years later. At this point Borges relates, in detail too complicated to be discussed here, how he came into possession of an even more mysterious work, a single volume of *A First Encyclopedia of Tlön* (Vol. XI, Hlaer to Jangr). Though only one tome of the *Encyclopedia of Tlön* could be located—even after such worthies as Alfonso Reyes, Ezequiel Martín Estrada, and Nestor Ibarra[18] are enlisted in the search for companion volumes—Borges finds enough material in the book to sketch out certain basic features of Tlönian culture. After explaining the "congenital idealism" of the planet, Borges discusses Tlön's languages in some detail. Because the Tlönian's basic worldview denies the existence of objects in space, there are no nouns in their languages; instead "there are impersonal verbs, modified by monosyllabic suffixes (or prefixes) with an adverbial value" (L, 8). Thus, Borges explains, they have no substantive for "moon," but rather a verb "to moon" ("lunar") or "to moonate" ("lunecer"); hence the sentence, "The moon rose above the river" is "hlör u fang axaxaxas mlö," or literally "upward behind the onstreaming it mooned" (L, 8). Tlönian science—what there is of it—is dominated by the planet's "classical" discipline, psychology. Because Tlönians have no conception of objects in space persisting in time, our notion of causality is nonexistent: "The perception of a cloud of smoke on the horizon and then of a burning field and then of the half-extinguished cigarette that produced the blaze is considered an example of the association of ideas" (L, 9). Moreover, Borges tells us, on Tlön every mental state is "irreducible"; hence the idea of classification suggests falsification and as a result "there are no sciences on Tlön, not even reasoning" (L, 10). Yet in a sense, there are sciences on Tlön, but such an infinitude of scientific systems exists that they are better thought of as individual "dialectical games." Neither Tlön's "scientists" nor its metaphysicians seek truth as we understand the term. Instead they seek "astounding" theories; as Borges puts it, the Tlönians have "an abundance of incredible systems of pleasing design or sensational type" (L, 10). A few misguided individuals insist on materialism and on systems that rest upon our usual notions of cause and effect. In a series of amusingly inverted paradoxes, Borges shows how Tlön's more sober minds have refuted these heresies.

Borges's analysis of Tlönian literary theories and practices is rich in self-caricature. We are informed that on Tlön books are not usually signed, for the idea "that all works are the creation of one author, who is atemporal and anonymous," seems to dominate literary attitudes. Plagiarism is, of course, a meaningless concept. "The critics often invent authors: they select two dissimilar works—the *Tao Te Ching* and the *Thousand and One Nights,* say—attribute them to the same writer and then determine most scrupulously the psychology of this interesting *homme de lettres*" (L, 13). Borges also notes that a favorite device in Tlönian fiction is the use of a single plot, but arranged in all its possible permutations.

Perhaps the most curious Tlönian phenomenon is the appearance of *hrönir,* that is, objects that are produced by various kinds of mental activity. As Borges blandly notes, "Centuries and centuries of idealism have not failed to influence reality" (*L,* 13). At first merely "accidental products" of distraction and forgetfulness, the *hrönir* were later deliberately produced. Thus Tlönian archaeologists who wish to prove a point simply *think* the necessary artifacts into existence.

The so-called postscript is devoted to a lengthy explanation of events and discoveries that supposedly take place between 1941 and 1944 and that shed light on the true authors of the *Encyclopedia of Tlön.* It seems that a seventeenth-century secret society dedicated to hermetic studies and the Cabala decided to "invent" a country. Although the original members of the group failed to carry out this objective, the society and their plan persisted. After a few centuries it sprang up again in the antebellum South of the United States. One Ezra Buckley, an eccentric millionaire of Memphis, Tennessee, whom Borges slyly describes in a footnote as a "freethinker, a fatalist, and a defender of slavery," becomes the patron of the resuscitated society. Buckley, who could easily have stepped out of the pages of *A Universal History of Infamy,* was apparently given to Gnostic heresies: he agrees to subvent the society's preparation of a forty-volume encyclopedia of the fictional planet provided "The work will make no pact with the imposter Jesus Christ" (*L,* 17). Evidently these terms were accepted, for many years after Buckley's demise (we are told, with no further explanation, that he was poisoned in 1828) the secret printing of the *Encyclopedia* was distributed to the society's members. Finally, Borges reports, in 1944 a complete forty-volume edition is discovered in the Memphis, Tennessee public library! The discovery of the *Encyclopedia*'s origins would seem to resolve all the questions that surrounded the apocryphal world of Tlön. But while Borges drops this veil of mystery he raises another. Inexplicable objects—a strangely heavy metal cone, a compass marked with the symbols of Tlön's alphabet—begin to appear. In short, a fantastic world intrudes on our world of reality.

If "Tlön" were to end at this point, which it does not, the reader would be confronted by a narrative structure rather typical of fantasy fiction, for beneath the philosophizing and games of the mind, a simple plot has unfolded. A person tells of a fantastic land whose puzzling existence is inexplicable; finally, its origins and true nature (a hoax perpetrated by a secret society) are revealed; and we breathe a sigh of relief only to discover that "real" objects from the nonplace have entered our own world. The pattern is similar to tales in which a narrator describes a crime of violence, then informs his reader that "it was just a dream," only to discover on awakening that a bloody dagger lies on the floor next to his bed.

But Borges steps back from this kind of conclusion to consider other possibilities. In a rather serious vein he notes that the world, on learning of Tlön and upon receiving the "corroborating" evidence of the strange objects noted above, seemed all too willing to "yield" reality to the attractive symmetry of this well-ordered planet: "The truth is that it longed to yield. Ten years ago any symmetry with a semblance of order—dialectical materialism, anti-Semitism, Nazism—was sufficient to entrance the minds of men.[19] How could one do other than submit to Tlön, to the minute and vast evidence of an orderly planet?" (L, 17) At the tale's conclusion Borges finds the world as he has known it slipping away: history is being rewritten, language is being transformed by the "conjectural, primitive" idiom of Tlön, and all fields of learning will soon be profoundly altered. In short, "The world will be Tlön." Despite the uncertainties of what is about to take place, Borges writes, "I pay no attention to all this and go on revising . . . an uncertain Quevedian translation (which I do not intend to publish) of Browne's *Urn Burial*" (L, 18).

"Tlön," then, may be approached in a number of different ways. On one level it is a sophisticated essay expounding certain favorite Borgesian themes; on another it is an almost classical tale of fantasy, featuring a kind of twist at the end that subverts the "explanation"; finally, it provides Borges with an opportunity to express some serious reactions to what has been happening in the real world of this century. Yet all these facets of the text are successfully unified by the central element: the discovery, the "explanation," and the final destiny of Tlön.

The Last Laugh: "Death and the Compass," "The Aleph," and "Pierre Menard, Author of the Quixote"

Although Borges may be taken very seriously, he remains a superb humorist. In fact he might well have been the greatest writer of humor to have appeared in Hispanic America before the "boom" of the 1950s. This may explain why early commentators often ignored or disliked his work, since until recently Spanish Americans have demanded an essential seriousness and propriety from their writers. At any rate, Borges's humor was evident in his earliest narrative work—*The Universal History of Infamy*, for example— and is present in a great many of the canonical texts. At times it takes the form of a single sly epithet in a serious context, at others it may appear as a quietly outrageous oxymoron, while in some pieces the better part of an entire text is revealed as a cosmic joke. Most important, while his is usually a gentle humor, it has an undermining, subversive quality. To borrow a phrase from J. D. Crosson, one of the few critics to have examined this essential facet of Borges's literary persona, it constitutes "a raid on the articulate."[20]

Cast as a detective story—one of Borges's favorite genres since his early readings of Chesterton—"La muerte y la brújula" ("Death and the Compass") is not especially unusual in its plotting. Reduced to essentials, it involves three apparent murders which occur at intervals of exactly one month apart and at locations which, when traced on a map, form an equilateral triangle. The supersleuth Erik Lönnrot is clever but not quite clever enough. He concludes that a fourth murder is to occur and that its time and place would be defined by forming a diamond-shaped figure on the base of the equilateral triangle. He traces the point on a map of the city and goes there exactly one month after the third murder. Lönnrot, hoping to forestall the crime and capture the killer, reaches the precise point indicated by his calculations, whereupon he is seized by two men, disarmed, informed in excruciating detail of how he has been lured to the spot, and then of course killed by his enemy the archcriminal Red Scharlach, alias "The Dandy."

The charm of the piece resides in its fundamental irony, in the interplay of Borgesian ideas, and in the tale's frequent sly bits of humor. The scene of the story is itself delightfully unlikely: a Talmudic congress at an unnamed French city that is, as Borges himself points out in one of his prologues, nothing more than a thinly veiled double of Buenos Aires. The characters in the tale are an equally unlikely group: the first victim, the scholarly rabbi of Podolsk, and student of Cabala, Dr. Marcel Yarmolinsky; the protagonist, the supersleuth Erik Lönnrot, a man of "reckless discernment"; Red Scharlach, author of the "fiendish series" of killings; the enigmatic third victim, one Ginsburg, also known as "Gryphius"; the innkeeper, Black Finnegan; various thugs, harlequins (the periods covered by the crimes includes Carnival); and a "myopic, shy atheist" who is the editor of the *Yidische Zeitung*. The two principal characters have names that tempt readers and critics into interesting speculations: why, for example, should the detective's name be Lönn*rot* (i.e., Lönn-*red*) and the criminal's name be *Red Scharlach* (Scharlach = Scarlet)?[21]

The device by which Lönnrot is duped could not be more Borgesian. The four points indicating the four "murders" (actually only three, since we learn at the tale's end that the third was a hoax) correspond to the mystic figure of the tetragrammaton, a Cabalistic emblem of the four Hebrew letters, JHVH, that make up the name of God. Scharlach, who is an old enemy of Lönnrot and who has sworn to kill him (this ridiculously obvious hint is given in the tale's first paragraph!) carefully designs the crimes knowing full

well that his enemy will follow all the deliberately placed clues and thus fall
into his trap. With infinite sangfroid, Scharlach tells his victim, just before
he shoots him, the details of the complex plan: "I . . . interspersed repeated
signs that would allow you, Erik Lönnrot, the reasoner, to understand that
the series was quadruple. A portent in the north, others in the east and west,
demand a fourth portent in the south. . . . I sent the equilateral triangle to
(Inspector) Treviranus. I foresaw that you would add the missing point . . .
the point which fixes in advance where a punctual death awaits you. I have
premeditated everything" (L, 86).

The ironies that underlie "Death and the Compass" should be obvious to
those who know Borges well. Note that Scharlach addresses Lönnrot as
"you, the reasoner." The detective is just that. Like most men who have faith
in reason, he attempts to find some scheme, some plan to his little universe;
but in trying to be clever he finds only defeat and death. As in "The Library
of Babel," as in "The Circular Ruins," or as in any number of other pieces,
Borges is again underscoring the theme of human vanity and futility. Perhaps the ultimate irony of "Death and the Compass" lies in the fact that the
very first "crime" was merely a mistake—Yarmolinsky was killed by a
drunken thug who was supposed to be robbing the room across the hall. In
this manner a *chance* happening provides the opportunity for Scharlach to
build his entire plot. Thus, even in the designs of the gods—for Scharlach in
his almost omnipotent manipulation of the situation seems to have godlike
powers—chance may well play an important role.

Despite these serious overtones, just as Scharlach has the last laugh on
Lönnrot, Borges seems to enjoy playing games with the reader. For example,
his use of triple motifs as opposed to quadruple elements, as when he names
the inspector *Tre*viranus or has the same character dismiss complicated solu-
tions to the crimes as "looking for a three-legged cat," is typical of his playful intercalation of hints and clues that become all too obvious in retrospect.

The title story of Borges's 1949 collection *El Aleph* (*The Aleph*) is another text that is often interpreted very seriously, if not solemnly, and yet is
extremely funny. The basic philosophical notion underlying it—the mystical identity of the macrocosm and the microcosm—is one that Borges had
explored in other pieces such as in his essay "The Fearful Sphere of Pascal"
and in one of the retold tales of the *Universal Infamy* collection, "The Mirror
of Ink."

Actually "The Aleph" is a curious hybrid. Although the last few pages
take up the question of the single small object that magically encompasses
the universe, more than half the text consists of a delightfully humorous
caricature or vignette of a certain Carlos Argentino Daneri, a contempo-

rary *porteño* (native of Buenos Aires), full of literary pretensions, verbose, and a complete bore, whose mental activity, writes Borges, "was continuous, deeply felt, far-ranging, and all in all, insignificant" (*AOS,* 17). For several pages Daneri annoys Borges by showing him selections of his verse—dreadful bits of doggerel from his epic description of the planet, modestly titled "La tierra." After each example of verse Borges is forced to listen to a long-winded justification of the particular selection: "I saw, however, that Daneri's real work lay not in the poetry, but in his invention of reasons, by which it should be admired" (*AOS,* 19). In view of Borges's verbal sensitivity, the fact that this half-baked literary buffoon should be named Carlos *Argentino* Daneri cannot be attributed to chance. Clearly Carlos is a caricature of some of the rather stupid, but nonetheless influential, members of Argentina's literary establishment. Even though "The Aleph" was written in 1945, it is quite possible that when Borges created Carlos Argentino he had in mind some of the jury that had denied him recognition in 1942. Support for this interpretation is found in the "postscript" to the story. Dated March 1943, this addendum explains how Carlos's magnificent literary efforts were crowned with the second National Prize for Literature whereas Borges's own "Los naipes del Tahur" ("The Gambler's Deck")—a nonexistant work, of course—did not even figure in the voting!

The apparently serious part of the story begins when Borges receives a frantic telephone call from Daneri. It seems that the venerable house of his parents and grandparents is about to be demolished and, with it, a priceless treasure. Argentino explains that in the basement of the house there is "an Aleph," without which he could not possibly write his monumental epic poem. Argentino further explains that "an Aleph is one of the points in space that contains all other points" (*AOS,* 23). Borges still doesn't quite understand, and so Argentino tells how he found it as a child, how it belongs to him, and how everything in the world is contained within it. Borges, his confusion compounded, decides to visit the house with Carlos to see for himself just what an "Aleph" might be. With Argentino as his guide, Borges descends the basement stairs, meticulously arranges himself and various objects according to the instructions of Argentino (whom he now fears may be a homicidal maniac), closes his eyes and then opens them.

At this point he sees the Aleph. Yet he complains, "here begins my desperation as a writer . . . how can I translate into words the limitless Aleph, which my floundering mind can hardly encompass?" (*AOS,* 26). He recalls that one ancient sage described this mystic point-which-is-all-points as "a sphere whose center is everywhere and whose circumference is nowhere," while other writers used different images. At any rate, despite the problems involved, Borges attempts a direct—and perhaps tongue-in-cheek— description of the Aleph and what he experienced by virtue of it: "On the back part of the stairway, toward the right, I saw a small iridescent sphere of almost unbearable brilliance. At first I thought it was revolving; then I realized that this movement was an illusion. . . . The diameter of the Aleph was probably little more than an inch, but, all space was there, actual and undiminished" (*AOS*, 26). Borges then devotes almost two pages to a fantastic enumeration of all that he saw in the Aleph. Among the infinitude of times are included "all the mirrors of the world and all without my reflection"; "a silvery spiderweb in the center of a dark pyramid"; "all the ants in the world"; "a beach along the Caspian Sea";[22] bison, tigers, obscene letters, and so on. In short, Borges remarks, he saw "the unimaginable universe" and felt "infinite wonder, infinite pity" (*AOS*, 28). At this dramatic moment he hears "a jovial and hateful voice": friend Argentino, calling from the top of cellar stairs, is inquiring if "Che Borges" enjoyed the spectacle and if he saw everything in color!

The contrast between the mystery and wonder of the Aleph's revelations and Argentino's banal comment is perhaps the most effective part of the story. More important, it serves to define the piece as an essentially humorous subversion of a philosophical notion. Borges often complained that he was taken too seriously: when writers criticize a story such as "El Aleph" on the ground that the fantastic elements in the piece are presented in an awkward or inept manner, they are doing precisely what Borges objects to. Taken as a serious example of fantastic fiction or as a solemn exposition of the mystical notion of the identity between the macrocosm and microcosm, the piece falls flat. Taken as a half-philosophical, basically playful composition—generously sprinkled with Borgesian irony and satire—"El Aleph" comes off rather well.[23]

Our examination of the canonical texts will close with the very first of the *ficciones*, the frequently cited "Pierre Menard, autor del Quijote" ("Pierre Menard, Author of the Quixote"). Its early date of composition (1939) notwithstanding, for many reasons "Menard" is a wonderful example of Borges's last laugh. The unnamed narrator, though he is often ignored by commentators, provides a masterful parody of the critical establishment; the central character (Menard can hardly be considered a protagonist) is one of the most cleverly conceived apocryphal figures in Borges's fiction; and finally the narrator's comment on Menard's principal achievement occupies that tenuous middle ground between high-powered critical intelligence and rampant sophisticated lunacy.

The overall framing device of the text, as perceptive readers soon discover, is a literary article appearing in a decidedly snobbish French journal. The first-person narrator affects the tone of a pretentious academic hack: his first task is to rectify certain unpardonable omissions "perpetrated" by another—and obviously less competent—student of Menard's work. After a paragraph of charmingly pompous name-dropping, the author presents a two-page bibliography of Menard's publications. Though completely apocryphal, the works listed show much internal consistency, bookish humor, and gentle irony. To appreciate fully Menard's far-ranging interests (chess, seventeenth- and eighteenth-century philosophy, French symbolism, and Paul Valéry), one must be a bit of an expert on these subjects, and on Borges as well. Not only does the author give us an enumeration of Menard's publications, but he even includes dates, footnotes, and the names of real journals in which he supposedly wrote. But all this is a mere preliminary. The main part of the piece describes Menard's writing of the *Quijote*—not just "another *Quijote* . . . but the *Quijote* itself." Menard's expression of this modest desire, as Borges reports it, is "My intent is no more than astonishing" (*L*, 39).

To prepare for this task, Menard first thinks of immersing himself in the world of Cervantes, of learning Spanish, of fighting the Moors, of recovering his lost Catholic faith, and of forgetting all the post-Cervantine history he had ever learned. Realizing the impossibility of this approach, he concludes that he would go on being simply Pierre Menard and would attempt, in some manner, to reach the *Quijote* through his own experiences.

At any rate, Menard writes his *Quijote* and Borges undertakes a close textual comparison of Cervantes' work with that of the Frenchman. The two texts, we are told, "are verbally identical, but the second is almost infinitely richer" (*L*, 42). Borges, half tongue in cheek, also points out that Menard's *Quijote* is more subtle and more ambitious than Cervantes' effort. After all, wasn't Menard a contemporary of William James and Bertrand Russell? And isn't Nietzschean influence clearly evident in his work? In the last few pages Menard's hazy existence is almost completely obscured by the provocative essayistic digressions Borges introduces. He concludes the piece with the thought that "Menard (perhaps without wanting to) has enriched, by means of a new technique, the halting and rudimentary art of reading: this new technique is that of the deliberate anachronism and the erroneous attribution" (*L*, 44). Finally, he suggests some possible applications of the technique: for example, why not attribute the *Imitation of Christ* to James Joyce, or why not consider the *Odyssey* as coming after the *Aeneid?* "Pierre Menard, Author of the Quixote" will strike those who are well grounded in literature, literary criticism, and Borges as clever, sophisticated, and quite funny. Others may find it dull, obscurely bookish, and quite pointless. The first group of readers will enjoy Borges's feigned pomposity, the inside jokes, the caricature of the literary world's petty feuds. They may also see a not-too-implausible reflection of Borges himself in Pierre Menard. Certainly the underlying ideas regarding the flow of time, authorship, plagiarism, and the philosophic interest in the contingent versus the necessary are Borges's as well as Menard's. Occasionally, an offhand remark describing Menard's personal quirks has a remarkably introspective ring. For example, Borges points out Menard's "resigned or ironical habit of propagating ideas which were the strict reverse of those he preferred" (L, 42). We are even more likely to make this association when Borges writes that Menard "decided to anticipate the vanity awaiting all man's efforts; he set himself to an undertaking which was exceedingly complex and from the very beginning, futile" (L, 43–44).

Anyone who has the temerity to write about Borges's "Pierre Menard" (or the work of any great author, for that matter) will, of course, run the risk of doing just what the story's pompous, self-important narrator attempted, namely, to seek fame and recognition vicariously through association with "the great man." Thus the text's main thrust may well be the subversion of the critical act itself. Details such as Menard's unwitting creation of a new technique of literary analysis, the bizarre and pretentious "deliberate anachronism and erroneous attribution," support this view. In sum, if this is his message to critics and scholars Borges has indeed had the last laugh.

Chapter Three
A Late Harvest

Any general assessment of a writer, especially of one who has had a long and fruitful life, invites us to consider his works in terms of developmental phases, of literary periods. Categories of this sort are of course quite arbitrary, but they do have some value in organizing the overall perspective of literary accomplishment. What constitutes Borges's early or formative period has been discussed in chapter 1: these years, from about 1923 to the 1940s, were dominated by an intensive poetic production, considerable essayistic writing, and the hesitant beginnings of work in fictional narrative. The second period, roughly from the late 1930s to the early 1950s, has been examined in chapter 2 in terms of what I call his canonical texts: this was a time of vigorous activity in prose fiction that produced what many deem his most important work; during these years Borges wrote a limited number of essays and relatively little poetry. The late 1950s and much of the 1960s appear to mark a hiatus in his activity: with the exception of one major collection, *El hacedor* (*Dreamtigers,* 1960), his total literary production declined substantially. In my preface I have already alluded to the remarkable renaissance of the 1970s. It is the work of these last decades of Borges's life—poetry, narratives, and miscellaneous prose—that constitutes the focus of this chapter. As for the biographical facts of this final period, little need be said. By the mid-1950s, with the demise of the Perón regime, intellectuals could once again breathe freely.[1] No longer would writers and academics be harassed, and ridiculed, as was Borges himself when, in 1946, Perón named him Inspector of Poultry and Rabbits—a "post" he had to officially renounce. Borges himself was officially recognized by the new democratic government, which named him director of the National Library. His growing literary fame, especially abroad, helped make life easier. From the 1960s on he settled into a pattern that remained virtually unchanged until his death: writing, work at the Library, occasional teaching, lecturing at distinguished universities, and travel. This essentially uneventful life was punctuated by a few significant events—his unsuccessful three-year marriage to Elsa Astete Millán (1967–70) and his second marriage, only a few months before his death, to his companion María Kodama.[2]

Dreamtigers

Whether *Dreamtigers* is considered a transitional work or the initial expression of Borges's final literary period, the collection is unique for several reasons. For one thing, it combines poetry and prose in one volume, a format that Borges was to use later on occasion. Second, its individual compositions, especially the prose pieces, are gems of minimalist art: they range from a few lines to a page or two at most. Perhaps most important, *Dreamtigers* is the first of several collections that Borges considered to be a summation of his literary achievement,[3] or, more accurately, an exorcism, "a liberation from former limitations, vanities and prejudices,"[4] to quote the critic Miguel Enguidanos. The same commentator even reports that Borges—at least in 1961—felt that this work would render his earlier efforts, notably *Fictions* and *The Aleph*, "unnecessary" (*Dt*, 10). In short, *Dreamtigers* may signal the shift away from the erudite literary gamesmanship and noonday brillance of the canonical texts toward the more somber allegories and autumnal hues of Borges's later period.

Although it appears easy to separate the prose from the poetry of *Dreamtigers,* taken as an integral work, the volume's tone is essentially poetic. Thus many of the most effective prose pieces are neither narrative nor expository in nature; rather, they reveal an inner-directed authorial voice, a kind of lyrical monologue, or at times an intimate dialogue with an old friend or cherished ghost. The first text, "A Leopoldo Lugones" ("To Leopoldo Lugones"), illustrates this well. The author, upon entering "the Library" (since 1955 Borges had directed the National Library, a post held a half-century earlier by the poet Lugones) confesses that he feels the "enveloping serenity of order [and] time magically desiccated and preserved" (*Dt*, 21). In a dreamlike state he enters Lugones's office to present the poet a copy of "this book," hopefully for the poet's perusal. He concludes the three short paragraphs of the text by again addressing his long-dead mentor: "My vanity and nostalgia have set up an impossible scene. Perhaps so (I tell myself), but tomorrow I too will have died, and our times will intermingle and chronology will be lost in a sphere of symbols" (*Dt*, 21). Several other prose pieces reveal a similar mood. For example, the magnificent tribute to the blind Homer (*el hacedor,* the "maker" or "creator," par excellence), from which the collection takes its Spanish title, suggests, without the slightest note of vanity, that the destinies of all creative men—Borges included—obliterate the vast distances of the centuries. On reading it we almost feel that Homer is Borges and that Borges is Homer. A different mood pervades the very personal "Dreamtigers," the title piece of the English-language version of *El hacedor*. In this piece we find the author confessing that in his dreams he is still the four-year-old child who sketched pictures of Indian tigers in his book of English nursery rhymes.

One of the strongest currents flowing through *Dreamtiger*'s pages is that of intense self-awareness. Borges seems to be taking stock of his work, of his relationship to time and place, and, in broad terms, of himself. This thematic cluster is evident in the collection's prose as well as in its poetry. Often it takes the form of a sudden sense of what Hispanic writers term *otredad* ("otherness"): in Borges's case this seems to involve a process of getting "outside" himself and then examining his essential being as opposed to his "self" as defined by externals. An impressive expression of the theme is seen in the frequently anthologized prose text "Borges y yo" ("Borges and I"). From its thought-provoking title to its dramatic last sentence the piece develops a fascinating döppelganger. The first lines present the basic motif: "It's the other one, it's Borges, that things happen to. . . . News of Borges reaches me through the mail and I see his name on an academic ballot or in a biographical dictionary" (*Dt*, 51). The author's "other" has many of the same likes and interests of the genuine, inner "I," but only "in a vain way that converts them into attributes of an actor." This other Borges has perhaps written "some worthwhile pages," but these now belong to the general corpus of literary tradition (a basic Borgesian notion, incidentally) so that "I recognize myself less in his books than in many others." He concludes on a note that is difficult to characterize, but appears whimsical yet at the same time somber: "Thus my life is running away, and I lose everything and everything belongs to oblivion, or to the other one. I do not know which of us two is writing this page" (*Dt*, 51).

A number of the poems in *Dreamtigers* reveal a similar sharpened self-consciousness heightened by this sense of otherness. In "Los espejos" ("Mirrors"), for example, the poet confesses an inexplicable childish horror at the thought of "the other" who looks back at him from mirrors or other reflecting surfaces. A slightly different variation on the theme is seen in the first poem of the same collection, "Poema de los dones" ("Poem about Gifts"), where Borges describes his wanderings through the National Library. He thinks of others who have done exactly the same thing:

> As I walk through the slow galleries
> I grow to feel with a kind of holy dread
> That I am the other, I am the dead,
> And the steps I take are also his.
> Which of us two is writing now these lines?

Al errar por las lentas galerías
Suelo sentir con vago horror sagrado
Que soy el otro, el muerto, que habrá dado
Los mismos pasos en los mismos días.
Cuál de los dos escribe este poema?

(Dt, 55–56)

The "other" to whom he refers may be Borges himself, viewed as a kind of biographical datum, or it may be an earlier director of the library—Lugones or perhaps Paul Groussac, whom he mentions in the poem. Another possible interpretation stems from an idea frequently expressed in Borges's prose: that all men are each other, that when doing exactly what another person has done we are, in some mystical sense, that person.

Otherness and the related themes of identity and self-awareness are only a few of the many motifs that make *Dreamtigers* a rich and fascinating volume, despite its brevity. Borges's musings on his steadily worsening blindness crop up on occasion, as in the previously cited "Poem about Gifts" in which he speaks of God's irony which gives him, at the same moment, both "books" (that is, his post as National Librarian) and "the night." Memories of long-vanished friends and relatives also haunt *Dreamtigers,* as in the lovely sonnet "La lluvia" ("The Rain"), where the poet recalls the sound of his father's voice, or in the fine elegiac tribute to the Mexican humanist Alfonso Reyes, "In memoriam, A. R." Finally, the quintessentially lyric theme of time's ceaseless flow appears with some frequency in the collection. It dominates the hauntingly beautiful poem "Arte poética" ("Ars poetica"), the evocative strophes of "Adrogué," and the verses of "El reloj de arena" ("The Hourglass").

In sum, *Dreamtigers* affirms the primacy of poetry in Borges's scale of literary values. His comments in this regard, made a few years before the collection's publication, are significant: "I understood that poetry was forbidden to me except in flashes, and in flashes lost in my works. . . . I think that with the stories I write, and with the essays too, I give as much poetry as I can."[5]

Later Poetry

In 1964, Borges's publishers, the Buenos Aires firm of Emecé Editores, brought out a single volume *Obra poética* (Poetic works) that included, with some modifications, his three early collections (discussed in chapter 1) and a group of mostly newer compositions under the subheading "El otro, el mismo" (The other, himself).[6] This section of the volume also includes the poems of *Dreamtigers,* though they are not identified as such. In addition, the collection retrieves a few poems from the forties and early fifties that had not appeared in earlier poetic collections. The 1979 *Obra poética* uses the same subtitle, "El otro, el mismo," for a section of the volume but adds a new prologue and a number of poems written in the late 1960s while it excludes the material from *Dreamtigers.* The same volume also includes a short collection of folkloric poetry, *Para las seis cuerdas* (For the six strings, 1965), *In Praise of Darkness* (1969), the poetry from *The Gold of the Tigers* (1972), *La rosa profunda* (The profound rose, 1976), and *La moneda de hierro* (The iron coin, 1976). The *Historia de la noche* (History of the night) appeared late in 1977 and is not included in the 1979 *Obra poética.* Borges's last two collections of poetry, *La cifra* (The cipher) and *Los conjurados* (The plotters), were published in 1981 and 1985 respectively.

It was seen earlier that after the mid-1930s, following a decade of prolific work in the genre, Borges's poetic activity was apparently declining. Yet a few poems of these years must be briefly noted: "La noche cíclica" ("The Cyclical Night"), a philosophical piece on the idea of cyclical history; "Del infierno y del cielo" (Of heaven and hell), a poem that signals Borges's growing fascination with *otredad,* a theme that came into full flower in *Dreamtigers;* and the dramatic "Poema conjetural" ("Conjectural Poem"), one of Borges's personal favorites. "Mateo XXV, 30" ("Matthew XXV:30") is another piece that serves to introduce the later poetry and also to underscore the importance of poetry in Borges's life. In it he likens himself to the foolish virgins in the parable of the ten talents. Though he has been given everything, all the raw material a poet might desire, "Stars, bread, libraries of East and West / . . . a human body to walk with on the earth / . . . algebra and fire" ("Estrellas, pan, bibliotecas orientales y occidentales / . . . un cuerpo humano para andar por la tierra / . . . algebra y fuego"), a voice tells him "You have used up the years and they have used up you, / and still, you have not written the poem" ("Has gastado los años y te han gastado, / Y todavía no has escrito el poema").[7]

By the mid-1960s Borges seems to have regained considerable momentum as a poet. Both thematically and technically his work displays a richness not seen since the 1920s. Although he appears to have acquired new interests, such as ancient Norse and Anglo-Saxon culture, older preoccupations persist, such as his unceasing infatuation with his native city and the history of his family. Certainly history, viewed at times in the microcosm of a small but crucial event, and at other times in broad sweep, remained a central concern. Closely related to his interest in the specifics of history is his constant fascination with time. And perhaps at the very root of all these concerns is a notion that recurs almost obsessively in his poetry as well as in his prose: the idea of the world as a complex enigma, expressed at times in the form of a labyrinth, or as the dream-made-real of a capricious creator.

On the technical side, a few generalizations can be made regarding the poetry of this later period. One of these is that while Borges never abandoned free verse and experimental forms, he shows an increasing tendency to use traditional metric patterns, notably the sonnet (in both its English and Italianate forms) and the hendecasyllable, especially as used in rhymed *cuartetos* (quatrains). Borges frequently stated that his fondness for more structured verse stemmed, at least in part, from the fact that it was easier for a nearly blind person to write poetry in these forms because it required less dependence on a visual text.

The first separately published poetry collection of the sixties is, in a sense, an anomaly. *Para las seis cuerdas* consists of only eleven compositions, all cast as lyrics of *milongas,* an Argentine musical form of the recent past. These pieces are written in strongly accented octosyllabic verse, hardly Borges's favorite metrical vehicle. Yet their spirit and content could not be more Borgesian: they reflect, albeit in a ritualistic, stylized manner, the world of passion and violence that pervaded the Buenos Aires lower-class outer suburbs of a century ago. This is the same world that fascinated Borges in his earliest narratives such as "Streetcorner Man," and that would continue to haunt him in his prose of the seventies: a vanished no-man's-land where the pampa impinges on the city; where weapons appear to have a life of their own; and where neighborhood *compadritos* settle old scores in almost balletic knife fights. Note, for example a fragment from the "Milonga de Calandria" (Milonga about Calandria): "He wasn't one of those technicians / Who'd use a trigger to bet his life / The game that he enjoyed / Was the dance that's done with a knife." ("No era un científico de esos / Que usan arma de gatillo; / Era su gusto jugarse / En el baile del cuchillo"; *OP,* 310). Although they can hardly be considered examples of Borges's most important poetry, the *milongas* of this collection provide an impressive example of how a sophisticated poet can take full advantage of a rich folkloric tradition. Moreover, those who are fond of ancient ballads or who enjoy Argentina's gauchesque poetry will find *Para las seis cuerdas* especially satisfying.

It is more difficult to generalize about the other poetry of the decade. Leaving aside the *milongas,* the sixty-odd poems of the period constitute an album of Borges's wanderings both spiritual and real. Prominent among his concerns are such things as the world of ancient Norsemen and Britons,

comments on his favorite authors, his characteristic fascination with historical turning points, and the ever present evocation of old Buenos Aires.
Many of these apparently disparate themes are, however, quite similar in
underlying motif. For example, his near obsession with weapons, especially
swords and daggers that seem to have a mystically autonomy, is glimpsed in
the sonnet "A una espada en York" (To a sword in York) as well as in the
prose poem "El puñal" (The dagger). In one case the setting is ancient Britain, in the other it is the Hispanic world of Spain and Argentina, yet in both
pieces the weapons are underscored as "symbols and names" of heroic destinies. In "El puñal," especially, the idea of the weapon as an independent living thing is clear:

> It is more than a metallic artifact . . .
> it is in a sense eternal, this dagger
> that killed a man in Tacuarembó
> and the daggers that killed Caesar.
> It desires to kill, it wants to shed fresh blood.

> Es más que una estructura de metales . . .
> es de algún modo eterno, el puñal
> que anoche mató a un hombre en Tacuarembó
> y los puñales que mataron a César.
> Qiuere matar, quiere derramar brusca sangre.
>
> (*OP*, 281)

The same motif dominates the free-verse "Fragmento" (Fragment) in which
Borges evokes the sword of Beowulf, "una espada que será leal / Hasta una
hora que ya sabe el Destino" ("a sword that will be loyal / Until that hour
already known by Destiny"; *OP*, 228). The theme is further evidenced in
several pieces dealing with heroic deaths: the fine sonnet to the medieval
Icelandic leader Snorri Sturluson and the poem to a nameless casualty of the
American Civil War, "Un soldado de Lee" (A Soldier under Lee).

But not all the poetry of this period is centered on death or bloody
weapons. A number of finely wrought sonnets present vignettes of favorite
personages such as Emerson, Poe, Whitman, Cansinos-Assens, Heine,
Swedenborg, Spinoza, and Jonathan Edwards. Finally, several poems may
be described as purely lyrical in nature. Of these, two sonnets, one titled in
English, "Everness," and the other in German, "Ewigkeit," are particularly
striking. Both are structured around one of Borges's perennial concerns—
the timeless realm of memory. The first piece begins with the affirmation

"Sólo una cosa no hay. Es el olvido" ("Only one thing does not exist. It is forgetting"); almost the same verse appears in the first tercet of "Ewigkeit": "I know that one thing does not exist. It is forgetting" ("Sé que una cosa no hay. Es el olvido"; *OP,* 258–59). "Everness" is perhaps the more personal of these companion pieces, as it hints at a long-remembered love. The poet recalls a face "left" in the reflection of mirrors at twilight and then concludes in a lovely pair of tercets:

> And everything is part of that diverse
> Glass of memory, the universe;
> Whose arduous corridors are endless
> And whose doors close as you walk by
> Only on the other side of twilight
> Will you see Archetypes and Splendors.

> Y todo es una parte del diverso
> Cristal de esa memoria, el universo;
> no tiene fin sus arduos corredores
> Y las puertas se cierran a tu paso;
> Solo del otro lado del ocaso
> Verás los Arquetipos y Esplendores.
>
> (*OP,* 258)

Borges referred to his collection of 1969, *In Praise of Darkness,* as his "fifth book of verse" and he notes in his prologue that while some prose "coexisted" with the poetry, he would prefer that the volume be read as a book of verse. The fact that half a dozen very short prose pieces are included leads Borges to make some interesting observations regarding the fine line that divides prose from poetry: "It is often said that free verse is no more than a typographical sham; I feel an error lurks in this assertion. Beyond its rhythm, the typographical appearance of free verse informs the reader that what lies in store for him is not information or reasoning but emotion."[8]

And indeed it is poetic emotion that awaits us in this collection. For example, the title piece, though placed at the end of the volume, represents one of Borges's most lyrical moments. Musing on his age and blindness, he observes:

> My friends are faceless
> women are as they were years back.
> one street corner is taken for another,

on the pages of books there are no letters.
All this should make me uneasy,
but there's a restfulness about, a going back.

Mis amigos no tienen cara,
las mujeres son lo que fueron hace ya tantos años,
las esquinas pueden ser otras,
no hay letras en las páginas de los libros.
Todo esto debería atemorizarme,
pero es una dulzura, un regreso.

(*PD,* 125)

Then, after recalling the multitude of his life's memories, he concludes: "Now I can forget them. I reach my center, / my algebra and my key, / my mirror. / Soon I shall know who I am" ("Ahora puedo olvidarlas. Llego a mi centro, / a mi álgebra y mí clave, / a mi espejo. / Pronto sabré quien soy"; *PD,* 127). A number of other poems in this collection reveal similar lyrical richness coupled with strong personal references. "Junio, 1968" ("June, 1968"), for example, is another lovely free-verse piece in which the poet uses a third-person viewpoint to describe himself at the task of arranging books in his library. The scene is set in a "golden afternoon," and the subject, while lovingly handling each volume muses:

. . . Alfonso Reyes surely will be pleased
to share space close to Virgil
[to arrange a library is to practice,
in a quiet and modest way,
the art of criticism.]

. . . a Reyes no le desagradará ciertamente
la cercanía de Virgilio,
(ordenar bibliotecas es ejercer,
de un modo silencioso y modesto,
el arte de la crítica."

(*PD,* 71)

The poem ends on a touching personal note with Borges again recognizing his blindness, the fact that he can no longer fully appreciate the books he is handling, and, most important, that he will never produce *the* book," "the book which . . . might justify him" ("el libro que lo justificará"; *PD,* 71).

During the last decades of his life Borges did a considerable amount of traveling, and his poetry testifies to his odyssey. Not surprisingly, whether he writes of Cambridge, Israel, or Iowa, his reaction to these places is essentially internal rather than external. Yet the fact that he vaguely senses the reality of unfamiliar locales seems to activate his muse, producing some fine lyrical moments, filtered through a rich matrix of literary and personal recollection. Thus in the sonnet "New England, 1967" he writes:

> Any day now [we are told] snow will come
> and out on every street America
> awaits me, but as evening falls I feel
> the slowness of today and the brevity of yesterday.
> Buenos Aires, yours are the streets that I
> go on walking without a why or when.
>
> Pronto (nos dicen) llegará la nieve
> y América me espera en cada esquina,
> pero siento en la tarde que declina
> el hoy tan lento y el ayer tan breve.
> Buenos Aires, yo sigo caminando
> por tus esquinas, sin por qué ni cuándo.
>
> (PD, 27)

The opposite perspective is seen in "Acevedo," a sonnet in which Borges celebrates a visit to his grandparents' property on the pampa and which brings to mind other similar regions he has known: "Plains are everywhere the same. I have seen / such land in Iowa, in our own south, in the Holy Land. . . . / That land is not lost. It is mine. I own / it in wistfulness, in oblivion" ("La llanura es ubicua. Los he visto / en Iowa, en el Sur, en tierra hebrea. . . . / No los perdí. Son míos. Los poseo / En el olvido, en un casual deseo"; PD, 81).

With regard to meter, throughout the collection the sonnet vies with free verse, with the former often used for pieces stressing external description and the latter for more intimate, confessional lyrics. Although this is far from an invariable relationship, it does account for a goodly number of the collection's poems. Some support for this notion may be seen in the unusual coupled pieces on the famous Dürer engraving, "Dos versiones de 'Ritter, Tod and Teufel' " ("Two Versions of 'Ritter, Tod and Teufel' "). In the first version, a sonnet, the graphic work is described in firmly drawn "objective" terms; in the second, consisting of twenty-two unrhymed hendecasyllables, Borges writes of "the other path" suggested by the knight's journey, that is, his own path, his own mortality.

The many canonical themes that run through *In Praise of Darkness* and the familiar ghosts that haunt its pages cannot be adequately treated in this brief discussion. In addition to the motifs noted here, the rich sampling of Borgesian preoccupations found in the volume would include the metaphor of the labyrinth, Heraclitus's river of time, the *Rubaiyat,* and of course Buenos Aires with its *compadritos,* knife fights, and passions.

In his 1972 prologue to *The Gold of the Tigers* Borges wrote that "for anyone who has lived out seventy years . . . there is little to hope for except to go on plying familiar skills, with an occasional mild variation and with tedious repetitious."[9] This very modest assessment of the collection may be, to a degree, accurate, yet Borges certainly made a fine art of variation on familiar themes—itself the very essence of great literature, as he so often suggested. A good example is seen in the rich hendecasyllables of "Cosas" ("Things"), a rather long enumerative poem in which Borges lists, with much fondness, those things that have been forgotten, that become invisible under certain conditions, that exist unperceived, or that have only the most ephemeral life:

> The mirror which shows nobody's reflection
> after the house has long been left alone.
> . . . .
> The momentary but symmetric rose
> which once, by chance, took substance in the shrouded
> mirrors of a boy's kaleidoscope
> . . . .
> The colors of a Turner when the lights
> are turned out in the narrow gallery
> . . . .
> The echo of the hoofbeats at the charge
> of Junín, which in some enduring mode
> never has ceased, is part of the webbed scheme.
>
> El espejo que que no repite a nadie
> Cuando la casa se ha quedado sola
> . . . .
> La simétrica rosa momentánea
> Que el azar dio una vez a los ocultos
> Cristales del pueril calidoscopio.
> . . . .
> Los colores de Turner cuando apagan

Las luces de la recta galería

. . . .

El eco de los cascos de la carga
De Junín, que de algún eterno modo
No ha cesado y es parte de la trama.

(*GT,* 19–21)

The piece ends with a reference familiar to readers of Borges: "El otro lado del tapiz. Las cosas / Que nadie mira salvo el Dios de Berkeley" ("The other side of the tapestry. The things / which no one sees, except for Berkeley's God"). The appeal to Berkeleyan idealism no longer seems to be a philosophical concern; rather the concept has become a trope suggesting that vast obverse of reality that is best perceived poetically.

A somewhat similar mood prevails in another piece on a familiar theme: the sonnet "On His Blindness," wherein the poet is "unworthy" of direct perception of the real world yet may still savor the riches of literature. Formally the poem is a gem: few sonnets show a better relationship between octave and sestet, dramatically introduced by the verb "I am." Yet another magnificent reworking of an old theme is found in the free-verse composition "El centinela" ("The Watcher"). Here, as in several earlier texts, Borges is haunted by the ghostlike presence of his "otherness." The poem begins as daylight enters his room, bringing conciousness of the other Borges who not only "lurks" in the room's mirrors and other reflecting surfaces but who even "dictates to me now this poem, which I do not like" ("dicta ahora este poema, que no me gusta"; *GT,* 29). This is the same being whom, he confesses, has been rejected by several women and who has forced him into the difficult study of the Anglo-Saxon language. The poem concludes with a bitter irony that reveals Borges in a decidedly grim mood: "We know each other too well, inseparable brother. / You drink the water from my cup and you wolf down my bread. / The door to suicide is open, but theologians assert that in the subsequent shadows of the other kingdom, there will be I, waiting for myself" ("Nos conocemos demasiado, inseparable hermano. / Bebes el agua de mi copa y devoras mi pan. / La puerta del suicidio está abierta, pero los teólogos afirman que en la sombra ulterior del otro reino, estaré yo, esperándome"; *GT,* 29).

A number of pieces in the collection strike familiar chords for anyone who has read the earlier Borges. "Hengist quiere hombres (449 A.D.)" ("Hengist Wants Men, A.D. 449"), while celebrating Anglo-Saxon culture from the first Germanic invasions onward, affirms a tenuous line of historical determinism: the Jutish chieftan, Hengist, not only wanted men to capture Britain, but also was sowing the seeds for Shakespeare's literature, for Nelson's ships, and for Borges—the grandson of England's Fanny Haslam—to write his poetry. Several poems again evoke the world of Buenos Aires knife fighters, others sing of the gauchos, and a few stand out for their novelty. Among the latter we find a series of short poems cast in the form of the Japanese tanka, a topical piece on the first moon landing, a poem on the prehistoric cave art of Altamira. One of the most interesting of these atypical compositions is "Tú" ("You"), a poetic comment on the impersonality of contemporary life and death. The initial verse firmly asserts: "In all the world, one man has been born, one man has died" ("Un solo hombre ha nacido, un solo hombre ha muerto en la Tierra"; *GT*, 25). To consider people as masses, he asserts, represents only the "impossible calculations" of statistics. This one individual is Ulysses, Cain, Abel, or Darwin on the bridge of the *Beagle*. He is a dead soldier at Hastings, Austerlitz, or Gettysburg. He is also an anonymous patient dying in a hospital, a Jew in a gas chamber; in short, he is you or I. The impressive final verses disproves the charge that Borges was an unfeeling intellectual lacking in human warmth: "One man alone has looked on the enormity of dawn. / One man alone has felt on his tongue the fresh quenching of water, the flavor of fruit and of flesh. / I speak of the unique, the single man, he who is always alone" ("Un solo hombre ha mirado la vasta aurora. / Un solo hombre ha sentido en el paladar la frescura del agua, el sabor de las frutas y de la carne. / Hablo del único, del uno, del que siempre está solo"; *GT*, 25).

The mid-1970s was a period of considerable poetic production for Borges. Moreover, the three volumes of verse that were published between 1975 and 1977, *La rosa profunda, La moneda de hierro,* and *Historia de la noche,* show little diminution of his lyric powers. The first collection, for example, presents several well-turned sonnets that have an almost Parnassian elegance: "La pantera" (The panther), "Habla un busto de Jano" (A bust of Janus speaks), or "El bisonte" (The buffalo). A striking experiment in this form is his Alexandrine sonnet, "La cierva blanca" (The white doe), a piece evidently inspired by a fleeting dream. He uses the same metrical scheme for another unusual poem in the second collection, "El ingenuo" (The simple soul). In this piece he confesses his wonderment at ordinary things rather than "marvels"—that a key can open a door, or that "the cruel sword can be beautiful / and that the rose has the fragrance of a rose" ("la espada cruel pueda ser hermosa, / Y que la rosa tenga el olor de la rosa"; *OP*, 486). These collections are especially rich in intertextual echoes. For example, the sonnet "Soy" (I am) ends on a note suggestive of the Baroque poetry of a

Góngora or Sor Juana: "I am an echo, a forgetting, nothing" ("Soy eco, olvido, nada"; *OP.*, 434). And of course there are the innumerable intratexts— poems whose subjects elicit reverberations of Borges's own poetry of prose: ancient Norse warriors, mirrors, coins, and old-time knife fighters like Juan Muraña.

Although Borges's poetry of this period remains impressive in terms of its quality as well as quantity, it is colored by a growing preoccupation with death and general pessimism. Aside from the obvious—that he was growing older—a number of other factors may explain this mood: the ill health and subsequent death of his mother and the brief return of Perón along with the continuing failure of Argentine democracy are a few of these. The bare-boned eleven-line free-verse poem "El suicida" (The suicide) is a particularly strong indicator of his frame of mind:

> I shall die and with me the sum
> Of the intolerable universe.
> . . . .
> I am looking at the last sunset
> I hear the last bird.
> I bequeath nothingness to no one.
>
> Moriré y conmigo la suma
> Del intolerable universo.
> . . . .
> Estoy mirando el último poniente
> Oigo el último pájaro.
> Lego la nada a nadie.
>   (*OP,* 430)

The theme of his blindness, which in earlier poems often functioned in a positive manner, now contributes to this autumnal gloom. Thus in the two-part composition "El ciego" (The blindman) he speaks of his "insipid universe," of being "deprived of the diverse world," and finally of how now "I can only see to see nightmares" ("solo puedo ver para ver pesadillas"; *OP,* 450). Yet a kind of sweet sadness pervades such pieces as the nostalgic "All Our Yesterdays," "Elegía" (Elegy), "La clepsidra" (The hourglass), and the enumerative poem "Talismanes" (Talismans). In the latter piece, after fondly recalling old friends, cherished objects, and pleasant experiences, he concludes in chilling tones: "Surely they are talismans, but they are useless against the shadow that I cannot name, against the shadow that I must not name" ("Ciertamente son talismanes, pero de nada sirven contra la sombra

que no puedo nombrar, contra la sombra que no debo nombrar"; *OP,* 459).
A somewhat similar mood pervades the poems of his 1977 collection,
Historia de la noche. Among a number of memorable lyrics at least one
must be briefly noted. In the English-titled "Things That Might Have
Been" he considers the possibility of such things as books that Dante might
have written after finishing the *Divine Comedy,* of the course of ancient history had the beautiful Helen of Troy not existed, and of other literary or historical events that did not come to pass. He concludes this enumeration of
"what might have been" when, in a striking final verse, he sadly thinks of
"The son I never had" ("El hijo que no tuve").[10]

In the prologue to his penultimate book of verse, *La cifra,* Borges discusses "verbal" poetry as opposed to "intellectual" poetry. To illustrate the
two he cites first the hauntingly lyrical first strophe of Ricardo Jaimes
Freyre's "Peregrina paloma imaginaria," and then the essentially intellectual
verse of Luis de León's "Vivir quiero conmigo."[11] He states that his desire in
this collection is to follow a middle course between these two extremes. How
successful he is in achieving this objective is difficult to determine. What is
clear, however, is that the collection is rich in opposing elements. At times its
tone is serene and hopeful while at other times death, desperation, and ni-
hilism hold sway. As to form, the sonnet gives way, with but one exception,
to free verse, prose poems, or the unrhymed hendecasyllable. Thematically,
a great deal of the collection is simply a reworking of well-known Borgesian
motifs, and by comparison with his earlier poetry these pieces on Berkeleyan
idealism, time, infinite regression, Buenos Aires, and so on are not especially
impressive. One relatively new theme does appear in several pieces: the culture and especially the literature of Japan. In *The Gold of the Tigers* he had
already experimented with the tanka form; here Borges presents, with considerable success, seventeen examples of the more familiar haiku. Several
other pieces on such subjects as the game of go, and the Shinto religion are
further indications of this interest.

On balance, however, the dominant mood of the collection is one of resigned weariness and melancholy, broken only occassionaly by a ray of sun-
shine. This is seen in any number of pieces. For example, in the title poem
he writes of the moon, "Has agotado ya la inalterable / suma de veces que
te da el destino. / Inútil abrir todas las ventanas / del mundo. Es tarde"
("You have already exhausted the unchangeable / sum of times destiny has
given you. / It is useless to open all the windows / of the world. It is late").[12]
An even more negative tone is evident in "Al adquirir una Enciclopedia"
(On acquiring an encyclopedia) in which the poet contrasts his joy and wonderment at having this new possession "with eyes that no longer function"

and hands that "fumble" through its illegible pages (*C,* 23). But perhaps
the most desperate poem in the collection, and yet one that contains some
lovely verses, is "Eclesiastés 1,9" (Ecclesiastes 1:9). He begins with a series
of strong hendecasyllablic lines, introduced by the word "if," that mention
simple everyday acts; he observes that *if* he does any of these things, he is
only repeating what he has done before. Borges then states, in the crucial
thirteenth verse: "No puedo ejecutar un acto nuevo, / tejo y torno a tejer la
misma fábula, / repetido un repetido endecasílabo" ("I cannot perform a
single new act, / I weave and re-weave the same tale, / I repeat a repeated
hendecasyllable"). He goes on to confess that night after night he has the
same nightmare and the same labyrinthine obsessions. The final verses are
especially dramatic: "I am the weariness of an unmoving mirror / or the
dust of a museum / I hope for only one untasted thing, / a gift, a bit of
gold in the shadows, that maiden, death" ("Soy la fátiga de un espejo
inmóvil / o el polvo de un museo. / Sólo una cosa no gustada espero, / una
dádiva, un oro de la sombra, / esa virgen, la muerte"; *C,* 27–28).

    Borges's last collection of poetry, *Los conjurados,* is signed 9 January
1985, a year and a half before his death. Like the previous volume, it is
dedicated to María Kodama, the woman who was to become his bride just
before his passing. Again, like *La cifra,* the volume includes some fourteen
short prose pieces, or about a third of its content. Some of these texts are
reminiscent of the parables written years earlier in *Dreamtigers,* and because
some of the poems are in blank verse, the fine line between prose and poetry
is not always easy to establish. There are, nonetheless, a goodly number of
sonnets and even a few octosyllabic *milongas* in the collection.

    In one of the shorter prose pieces, "Posesión del ayer" (Possession of yes-
terday), while pondering the notion that in a sense what we lose is often retained in a special way, Borges remarks, "Every poem, with time, becomes
an elegy."[13] This observation certainly applies to many of the collection's
pieces. One of the many cases in point is the lovely poem "La joven noche"
(The young night). The tone here is one of gentle acceptance; the twilight of
life reduces the world to pure essences, to Platonic ideas. Citing a favorite
author Borges comments: "Goethe said it better: *nearby things became distant.* / There four words sum up all twilight. / In the garden the roses stop
being roses / and wish to be the Rose" ("Mejor lo dijo Goethe: *Lo cercano se
aleja.* / Esas cuatro palabras cifran todo el crepúsculo. / En el jardín las
rosas dejan de ser las rosas / y quieren ser la Rosa"; *Co,* 29). A somewhat
similar mood pervades poems such as "Doomsday" or "Tríada" (Triad). The
latter, a fine example of free-verse innovation, is built upon three statements, each a bit longer than its predecessor and each describing the "alivio"

(relief) felt immediately before death. The first two statement—or verses—speak of famous men such as Caesar or Charles I or England. The final segment, however, is expressed in personal terms as "The relief that you and I will feel at the moment preceding death, when fortune casts us free of the sad habit of being someone and of the weight of the universe" ("El alivio que tú y yo sentiremos en el instante que precede la muerte, cuando la suerte nos desate de la triste costumbre de ser algiuen y del peso del universo"; *Co,* 20). The very fact that Borges, then eighty-five, was still exploring that fascinating no-man's-land between prose and poetry, was still writing fine sonnets, and was continuing to rework the rich metal of earlier texts suggests that even though death was close, he remained a poet of substantial talent and considerable vigor.

Later Prose

While specialists and Borgephiles will always be impressed by his poetry, the general reader usually thinks of Borges first and foremost as a matter of prose fiction. I suspect that this will prove as true with regard to his work of the seventies and eighties as it was regarding his earlier writings. Two major collections of stories appeared during the last quarter century of Borges's life: *Doctor Brodie's Report* (1970) and *The Book of Sand* (1975). Some prose is also to be found in *The Gold of the Tigers* and *Los conjurados,* but these are essentially poetry collections and the very short sketches or parables in them have only slight narrative interest. Two additional works might be added to the titles noted: *Veinticinco de agosto 1983 y otros cuentos* (The twenty-fifth of August 1983 and other stories, 1983), a short volume of which only the title story had not been published elsewhere; and the thirty-four-page *Rosa y azul* (Pink and blue, 1977), containing only two stories, both of which reappear in *Veinticinco de agosto 1983*. It is of some interest that of the approximately thirty-five pieces of prose fiction found in all these collections, all but three had been written by 1975.

As noted earlier, the prologues Borges wrote to accompany his books can be disarmingly candid. Thus he introduces *Doctor Brodie's Report* by observing that "Kipling's last stories were no less tormented and mazelike than the stories of Kafka or Henry James . . . but in 1885, in Lahore, the young Kipling began a series of brief tales, written in a straightforward manner." He goes on to state that some of these stories are "laconic masterpieces" and that it has occurred to him, though he was now an old writer, to attempt something similar. He then says of his latest collection: "I have done my best—I don't know with what success—to write straightforward stories. I do not dare state they are simple; there isn't anywhere on earth a single page or single word that is, since each thing implies the universe, whose most obvious trait is complexity."[14]

A good example of these deceptively "straightforward" tales may be seen in "La intrusa" ("The Intruder"), the first story of the Spanish edition and also the first of the collection in terms of its date of composition. A superificial reading of this piece might suggest that it was the work of another writer, certainly not the Borges of *Ficciones* and *The Aleph*. The story line consists of a simple, bare-bones narrative: Cristián Nilson, one of a pair of tough, red-haired brothers who live in a small rough town on the edge of Buenos Aires, takes up with a dance hall girl who comes to live with him and his brother. In time, Cristián invites the younger Eduardo to "share" Juliana with him. This arrangement continues for a while, but the girl's preference for Eduardo creates tensions that are resolved by selling her to the madam of a nearby brothel. The brothers attempt to forget her by returning to their earlier days of carousing together. But one day Cristián finds out that his brothers has been visiting Juliana at the brothel, and to avoid further problems they decide to take her back home. At the end Cristián kills the girl, and the two throw her unburied body out on the pampa for "the buzzards to take over." The brothers embrace and the narrator notes that now "one more link bound them . . . the woman they had cruelly sacrificed and their common need to forget her" (*BR*, 68).

Like most of the stories in *Doctor Brodie's Report*, "The Intruder" had, at least on the surface, very little resemblance to the canonical texts. There were no playful, erudite references to writers or philosophers, humor was absent, and the story itself—revolving around crudeness, sex, and prostitution—was hardly reminiscent of the Borges of earlier years. Yet there may be more here than meets the eye: for one thing, the relationship between the brothers echoes, to a degree, the biblical polarity of Cain and Abel. Although the tale seems to end on a note of fraternal conciliation, a sly comment at the very beginning of the text casts some doubt on the true relationship. Borges notes that the younger brother, Eduardo, who "probably" first told the story, had reported, somewhat vaguely, that Cristián "had died in his sleep sometime back in the nineties" (*BR*, 63). Given the fact that Eduardo was the first to "cheat" on his brother and that Cristián actually murdered the girl, one wonders about the true circumstances surrounding the older brother's death. Thus, at least a shadow of fratricide haunts the tale. This interpretation, suggesting an allegory or a parable, is further supported by the stark prose of the piece. Borges, moreover, gives the text a kind of mythic quality by his deliberate use of a diffuse narrative frame. The first line, for example, reads "People say (but this is unlikely) that the story was first told by Eduardo. . . . The fact is that someone got it from someone else. . . . Years later, in Turdera, where the story had taken place, I heard it again" (*BR,* 63). In short, this is hardly as "straight-forward" a tale as Borges would have us believe.

Similar in some respects to "The Intruder," "El evangelio según Marcos" ("The Gospel according to Mark") has probably attracted more attention than any other story in *Brodie.* However, in this case the biblical parallel is not merely suggested, it is in fact quite obvious. The third-person authorial voice, too, is very direct, almost laconic in its short declarative sentences, with no attempt to diffuse sources or to rely on second-degree narrators. The story begins when Baltasar Espinosa, a kindly, rather ordinary medical student from Buenos Aires, arrives at a ranch out on the pampa for a brief vacation. His cousin, the owner, must go off on business, leaving Espinosa with the foreman Gutre and the latter's son and daughter. Though of mixed Scottish-mestizo blood, the red-haired Gutres have over generations become rather primitive, even to the point of illiteracy. Yet they are fascinated by the old family Bible—one of the few books in the house—and during a rainy week late in March they listen en-tranced as Espinosa reads aloud their favorite text: the account of Christ's crucifixion in Mark. On Thursday night of that week, after the customary reading of this text, Espinosa retires only to be awakened hours later by Gutre's daughter. Naked and silent she enters his bed, gives herself to him, and leaves. We are not even told the girl's name. The following day the Gutres ask Espinosa if salvation was extended to the soldiers who nailed Christ to the cross, to which he replies affirmatively. Toward evening—Friday, it should be noted—the Gutres approach him and ask his blessing: "Then they mocked . . . him, spat on him, and shoved him to the back part of the house. The girl wept. Espinosa knew what awaited him on the other side of the door." The tale ends ominously as the narrator describes the scene: "The shed was without a roof; they had pulled down the beams to make a cross" (*BR,* 21–22).

Even before this dramatic denouement, the parallels with the New Testa-ment are abundantly clear: Espinosa's age (thirty-three); his given name (*espinosa* literally means "thorny"); his mild character; the fact that he is a medical student (that is, a "healer"); the time of the year; the day of the tale's climax—Friday; the role of the daughter, suggestive perhaps of Mary Magdalene; the way in which the Gutres pamper and revere Espinosa; and a number of other minor details. Yet Borges makes it difficult for his readers to accept the tale as a purely symbolic modern recasting of the crucifixion.

Although at times the action takes place as if in a world of dreamlike ritual, the author gives many very down-to-earth details regarding such things as Espinosa's friends back in Buenos Aires, ordinary life on the ranch, the exact location of the property, among others. Thus one is tempted to agree with one critic who dismissed "The Gospel according to Mark" simply as a story in which "a rather naive student reads the Bible to a family of degenerate and illiterate Calvinists only to discover . . . that they take the story of Jesus' crucifixion too literally."[15] If this is indeed its main point, then it must be considered a rather shallow tale, clearly inferior to the canonical stories. Other critics, however, have found rich intratextual echoes in the piece that shed light on Borges's older work as well as on this text itself. Carter Wheelock, for example, relates the work to Borges's provocative notion that all fiction may be variations on only two related themes—the "voyage of men lost in chaos" and the "exaltation through death . . . of a supreme centrality on Golgotha."[16] It may also be a reworking of the Borgesian preoccupation with obsessive objects, seen here in the Gutres' "holy obsession" with Christ. Other aspects of "The Gospel" are more difficult to explain: the strange incident of the Gutre girl's giving herself to Espinosa may symbolize a "gift" to the Master or a very tenuous parallel with the Magdalene's carnality. Like "The Intruder," "Emma Zunz," or the very early "Streetcorner Man," sex on occasion plays an important role in his fiction, yet when it surfaces, the language, by contemporary standards, is indirect, vague, and schematic. In short, the description of the Gutre girl's nocturnal encounter with Espinosa is an excellent example of the unsexy sex in Borges's writing.

Most of the other stories in *Brodie* are less problematic than "The Gospel"; yet only a few would convince readers that Borges was indeed following his new policy of writing "straightforward" prose. Among several pieces that deal with the theme of rivalry, at least two reveal sufficient literary gamesmanship to suggest that Borges's old habits persisted. The first text, "El duelo" ("The Duel"), is in some ways quite atypical. Its co-protagonists are female and are painters: one does fairly representational work whereas the other cultivates abstract art. On the more obvious level, the duel here revolves about the relative merits of the two kinds of painters; however, Borges insinuates several subplots—such as a possible rivalry between Clara, the abstract artist, and her sister Marta, the traditionalist, who had once been in love with Clara's husband. More like his earlier tales, "The Duel" contains a goodly number of literary references and even some half-serious asides, such as the comment that abstract artists, because they followed the Biblical injunction against making graven images, "were going back to the true tradition of painting, which had been led astray by such heretics as Dürer and Rembrandt" (*BR*, 37). Borges also uses the tale to make a number of ironic remarks about Argentine society, "where a woman is regarded as a member of the species, not an individual," and where aesthetic movements—such as abstract painting—are treated as the "latest rage" after they have run their course elsewhere.

In "Guayaquil" the theme of rivalry is double-layered: the primary plot centers on two historians who are in competition to be sent on an official mission to study important documents in a foreign capital. The two academics, though quite different in background, are in Argentina but the place they wish to visit is called "Sulaco, the capital of the Estado Occidental"—a Caribbean city that may suggest Caracas, Venezuela. The object of their interest is some recently discovered letters written by Simón Bolívar and dealing with his famous closed-door meeting with General San Martín, the leader of the revolutionary forces of the South during Spanish America's wars of independence. Although Borges briefly explains the Bolívar-San Martín confrontation of 1823 in Guayaquil, Ecuador, only those fully aware of the profound temperamental differences between the two and of the historical circumstances surrounding their meeting can fully appreciate the way that this event parallels and reflects the rivalry between Professor Zimmerman and the other, unnamed academic. The central question regarding the meeting that has puzzled experts and amateurs alike is how to explain San Martín's decision to defer to Bolívar. We do know that at Guayaquil the Argentine general backed off and shortly thereafter left South America for permanent exile in Europe; but was this owing to Bolívar's stronger will, to some secret plan of San Martín, or to a trap of some sort? At any rate, in the primary story the Argentine historian, through whose narrative voice the tale is told, apparently has just been named by the government to undertake this important mission. However, after a long conversation with Zimmerman—a recently arrived German-Jewish scholar who combines, according to his rival, "both Jewish and German servility"—the Argentine historian signs a letter, prepared in advance by his rival, declining the invitation to visit Sulaco. Thus, he leaves the honor to Zimmerman.

Aside from the main structural feature (the parallel rivalries of the two historians and the two soldiers), the piece is rich in intratexts and echoes that recall the Borges of earlier days. The polarity established between the two professors is certainly a canonical gambit. Zimmerman, though very clever, is in a sense a parvenu: Jewish, "immoderately" dressed, an exile from his native Prague, a speaker of "inelegant" Spanish, he stands in sharp contrast to the narrator who is of old Argentine stock, proud of his heritage, of his

family trophies, and of his ancestors who fought in the wars of independence. Yet through some inexorable force, perhaps his rival's sheer will, he
yields to Zimmerman. The charged atmosphere that develops at this cli-
mactic point in the story is described by the narrator in a tone reminiscent of
Yu Tsun's confrontation with Stephen Albert in "The Garden of the Forking Paths:" "At that moment I felt that something was happening between
us, or, rather that something had already happened. In some uncanny way
we were already two other people" (*BR*, 106). Here again Borges's fascination with that thin line that divides hero from traitor or victor from van-
quished is evident. There may be other ways of looking at this text: the
Argentine professor's deference to Zimmerman has an aesthetic dimension,
suggesting that his unexplained, indeterminate act creates an air of mystery
that yields better literature than would have been produced had he pursued
the project. This is a finespun interpretation, but one commentator, Carter
Wheelock, argues persuasively for it and supports his views with a number
of details from the text.[17]

Rivalry of a more basic sort characterizes another group of stories in this
collection. "El otro duelo" ("The End of the Duel"), "El Encuentro" ("The
Meeting"), "Historia de Rosendo Juárez" ("Rosendo's Tale"), and "Juan
Muraña" all describe violent encounters—knife fights especially—between
guapos (toughs) and their rivals. These tales have the same setting and ambience found in some of the poetry of the period, notably the *milongas*. A
recurrent theme here, as in their verse counterparts, is Borges's almost mystical reverence for weapons, especially knives and daggers that seem to have
a will or destiny of their own. Another interesting feature of these stories is
Borges's manipulation of his narrative frame. In all four, a second-level narrator tells the story: an old friend met on a train trip, a colorful *guapo* who
witnessed the events years before, the nephew of a long-dead knife fighter,
or a specific literary colleague who heard it from a third party. Often Borges
claims that he has found more than one version of the events or that his
memory may be faulty regarding some details. Why Borges so frequently
yields the floor to secondary narrators or deliberately plays the role of unreli-
able narrator remain interesting questions that cannot be fully resolved here.

Two pieces in *Doctor Brodie's Report* are unusual in terms of the
collection's dominant mood. The first of these, "La señora mayor" ("The
Elder Lady"), is more a vignette than a genuine story. In it Borges describes,
with considerable affection, the last days in the life of a woman of great dig-
nity whose one hundredth birthday is about to be celebrated. Because the
protagonist's distinguished family participated in the wars of independence,
she is treated as a national symbol and at her birthday celebration press and

government representatives make a great fuss over her. Though she is barely aware of what is going on and utters not a single word, the newspaper accounts of the affair speak of her wonderful memory and characterize her as "a storehouse of a century of Argentine history." Borges's concluding remarks suggest that she was the last victim of the wars of independence. In all probability, the implication here is that true love of country, authentic patriotism, is often subverted by overblown nationalistic rhetoric.

The second of these tales is the title piece, "Dr. Brodie's Report." Critical reception of this story has in general been rather negative: one commentator deems it "surely one of Borges's weakest single works,"[18] while others simply say little about it. The story—or report—consists of a fairly detailed description of a strange African tribe, whose unusual culture and customs give the piece an almost fantastic aura. Reminiscent of "Tlön" and earlier pieces, the report is framed, however, by Borges's "explanation" of how he came across the Brodie manuscript: it mysteriously turned up, missing its first page, among the leaves of a recently acquired edition of the *Arabian Nights Entertainments*. Not only this framing device but the general outline of the piece recall to some degree Borges's celebrated earlier story. The report, like the encyclopedia of Tlön, studies the language, religion, and values of a bizarre—though not quite fantastic—society that might conceivably have existed in the heart of darkest Africa. Brodie, a Scottish missionary, prefers to call these people "Yahoos," rather than the "Mlch" (their actual name), since he would remind us "of their bestial nature." The reference here to Gulliver is of course obvious; however, it serves to prepare the reader for the story's conclusion. In general, Brodie's Yahoos are an unattractive and strange lot: they are cannibals, go about naked, practice castration and amputation, are insensitive to pain or pleasure, are unimaginative, and have virtually no memory. Despite all this and despite the fact that their monosyllabic language has only generic nouns, they do seem capable of forming abstract ideas, which leads to the conclusion that "for all their backwardness [they] are not a primitive but a degenerate nation" (*BR*, 117). As Brodie concludes, he notes several other redeeming features that this essentially "barbarous" people possess. Yet the last line of the text is quite enigmatic: "it is my fervent prayer that the Government of Her Majesty will not ignore what this report makes bold to suggest." Given the oblique reference to Swift's term "Yahoo," one immediately thinks of the latter's well known *Modest Proposal*. Yet Brodie's final assessment of the Mlch—or Yahoos— seems at odds with anything so drastic as Swift's solution to the Irish problem. In short, this inconclusive ending (the absent "suggestion," one might assume, appeared in the missing page of the manuscript) does not seem especially clever. Like a number of rather pointless details in the body of the report, it lacks the provocative ambiguity so often found in Borges's best work.

There is little agreement regarding the merits and nature of the last of Borges's major collections devoted to fiction, *The Book of Sand*. For one critic the book is "unabashedly fantastic,"[19] for another it is an uneven, essentially weak volume.[20] The collection's largest and perhaps richest text, "El congreso" ("The Congress") has met with similarly mixed reactions. Published separately several years before *The Book of Sand* appeared, "The Congress" is laden with classically Borgesian characters, motifs, and preoccupations. This is not surprising because in interviews Borges frequently remarked that he had been working on it for several decades. In fact he dates it 1955, which, if taken at face value, places it close to the period of the canonical texts. The story's narrator, one Alejandro Ferri, is a partial double of Borges himself: born in 1899, he states that as a young man he "was fond of sunsets and slums," that he now teaches English to classes of only a few students, and that he is the author of a long-forgotten *Brief Analytical Examination of John Wilkins*. This apocryphal volume of course suggests Borges's early essay titled "The Analytical Language of John Wilkins," whose central theme figures prominently in "The Congress."

The title of the story derives from the fact that the plot—what there is of one—centers on the narrator's initiation into a secret society, the modestly named "Congress of the World," and his rather detailed description of the group's colorful membership and history. Perhaps the key scenes occur when one of the assemblage raises a "philosophical problem," namely, how this relatively small group could possibly represent all humanity. As the member observes, "planning an assembly to represent all men was like fixing the exact number of Platonic archetypes—a puzzle that had taxed the imagination of thinkers for centuries."[21] The astute reader of Borges immediately sees here the germ of a philosophical problem—or logical pastime— that had fascinated him since the twenties: the entire question of how the infinitude of the universe might be organized and classified. Much of his interest in language—the area of reality described by a single word, the relationship of generic to specific concepts, and the like—revolves about this central concern. It certainly shapes a number of the canonical stories ("Tlön," "Funes," "The Library of Babel," to mention a few), it is brilliantly formulated in the half-serious essay on John Wilkins's synthetic language (see chapter 1), and it has had an interesting impact on contemporary criticism, as will be noted in chapter 4. In "The Congress" it comes to the fore in the description of how various members of the society might represent the totality of mankind: "Alejandro Glencoe [the president] might represent not only cattleman but also Uruguayans, and also humanity's great forerunners, and also men with red beards, and also those who are seated in armchairs. Nora Erfjord was Norwegian. Would she represent secretaries, Norwegian womanhood, or—more obviously—all beautiful women? Would a single engineer be enough to represent all engineers—including those of New Zealand?" (*BS*, 34–35). This mad debate on taxonomic choices is, however, soon abandoned. In rapid succession the narrator describes a brief encounter with a knife fighter who threatens him as he leaves the meeting; an intense, hopelessly Borgesian discussion on the books to be selected for the society's library; a visit to Glencoe's ranch complete with picturesque gauchos and horses; and finally his trip to London where he takes rooms near the British Museum in order to to find in its library "a language worthy of the Congress of the World." Not surprisingly, he is especially taken with the possibility of using a synthetic tongue: Esperanto, Volapük, or our friend Wilkins's "analytic language."

As if all this were not enough, in the British Museum he meets the young and charming Beatrice Frost, with whom he promptly becomes enamored. Red-haired, northern, yet possessing more passion than her boreal surname might suggest, she refuses to marry Ferri, but does become his lover. Though he realizes that he may be straying from his objective of giving his readers an account of the Congress, he cannot resist describing this London idyll: "O nights, O darkness warm and shared, O love that flows in shadows like some secret river, O that instant of ecstasy when each is both . . . O the coupling in which we become lost . . . O the first light of dawn, and I watching her" (*BS*, 43). This attempt at a lyrical evocation of physical love is one of the least typical—and least effective—passages in the piece, if not in Borges's entire literary corpus.

At any rate, Ferri must return to Buenos Aires, his affair with Beatrice becomes just a fading memory, and the business of the Congress again takes center stage. It seems that the society, convinced that "there is no book so bad it does not contain some good," has acquired a rather disparate collection of items for its library: "bound volumes of the daily press, 3,400 copies of *Don Quixote* in various editions, the complete works of General Mitre, Ph.D. theses, old account books, bulletins, and theatre programs" (*BS*, 44). This strange collection has been stored in the cellar of Glencoe's house. As the narrative continues, Ferri tells of a raw evening at the latter's home when Glencoe has the books removed from the basement, piled high in the patio, and then burned. A member of the society thereupon solemnly remarks: "Every few centuries . . . the Library of Alexandria must be burned down."

Glencoe then adds his own enigmatic revelation: "The Congress of the World began with the first moment of the world and it will go on when we are dust. There's no place on earth where it does not exist. The Congress is the books we've burned. The Congress is Job on the ash heap and Christ on the Cross. The Congress is that worthless boy who squanders my substance on whores" (BS, 47). In other words, like the library in "The Library of Babel," the "Congress" signifies the universe. The story ends with the group taking a lighthearted spin around the city and with the narrator's offhand remark that "what really matters is having felt that our plan, which more than once we made a joke of, really and secretly existed and was the world and ourselves" (BS, 49).

If "The Congress" was meant to be taken seriously, it is a rather weak hodgepodge of themes and motifs many of which had been articulated better in other texts. If, however, it is taken as another example of Borges's last laugh at critics, scholars, and perhaps even the general reader, it comes off quite well. My own reading of it favors the latter interpretation. There are too many embedded tricks, cutely placed intratextual references, familiar names, and echoes of points that have intrigued his commentators for years for us to assume that its author was not being very deliberate in "setting us up," as it were, for this funhouse of Borgesiana.[22]

The other stories in The Book of Sand are shorter than "The Congress" and, in most cases, less complex. Two of them, "Ulrica" and "La noche de los dones" ("The Night of the Gifts"), involve important female characters and illustrate the same pale, ritualistic eroticism noted in the Beatrice Frost interlude of "The Congress." In "Ulrica," the narrator (a "Colombian" academic visiting Britain and another quasi double of Borges) falls in love with a mysterious, willowy girl whom he meets in York. In the course of their encounter they speak of the ancient Norse invasion of England and she refers to herself as Brynhild and to him as Sigurd. Several other details such as the howl of a wolf (an animal long extinct in modern Britain), heard as they walk through snowy woods, establish a kind of temporal fusing. The tale ends with the two consummating their love in a cozy upper room of "The Northern Inn": "Time passed like the sands. In the darkness, centuries old, love flowed, and for the first and last time I possessed Ulrica's image" (BS, 25). In a very different kind of story, "The Night of the Gifts," a sexual encounter also plays a central role. In this case an aging narrator recalls how, as a thirteen-year-old, he lost his virginity in a small-town brothel and during the same night witnessed a killing. Though the circumstances are quite different, the reader is again struck by the half-real, half-ritualistic description of the act of love: "I have no idea how much time passed. We exchanged neither a word nor a kiss. I untied her braid, and my hands played with her hair, which was very straight, and then they played with her. We did not see each other again after that, and I never learned her real name" (*BS*, 72). The question of why Borges chooses to link the two events (the sexual encounter and the killing) is an intriguing detail but one that will not be pursued here. At any rate, the prostitute who initiates the young lad is anonymous; she is simply known as "La Cautiva" (the Captive), a nickname that evokes, at least for Argentine readers, a literary echo of early romantic poetry. Like the almost unobtainable, cooly named Beatrice Frost of "The Congress," or the tall blond Ulrica/Brynhild of "Ulrica," the Captive says little, is never seen again, and appears to move in a mythic realm rather than in the real world.

Given the facts of Borges's life, there is a great temptation to submit this late-blooming eroticism to psychoanalytic scrutiny. It is true that eroticism, though suppressed in many ways, can be found just below the surface of his earlier poetry and in some of his fiction. Critics have been aware of its presence. Rodríguez Monegal, for example, has written: "It has always been hidden or disguised, masked or displaced. In his late seventies he has allowed himself finally to admit in print the validity of erotic dreams."[23] There may be more here than just giving literary form to erotic dreams: his extremely close relationship with his mother who died only in 1975, his occasional but apparently platonic affairs with women, and his late but unsuccessful first marriage, along with several recurrent motifs in his work having marked sexual connotations, invite those who are fascinated by Freudian criticism to pursue this approach.

Of the remaining stories in *The Book of Sand* little need be said, because they are essentially reworkings of familiar themes often presented more effectively in earlier texts. "El otro" ("The Other") revolves around intersecting temporal planes: in it Borges, a first-person narrator, tells of his meeting with a young man who turns out to be himself as a youth in his late teens. The possibility that the "elder Borges" was simply dreaming the "young Borges," or vice versa, is suggested. There are a number of references that link the piece to other texts, but on balance it does not quite come off. Two stories, "There are more things" and "Utopía de un hombre cansado" ("Utopia of a Tired Man"), border on the fantastic or the realm of science fiction: neither seems especially effective. "El soborno" ("The Bribe") is of some interest because, like "Guayaquil," it deals with rivalry among academics; the earlier piece, however, has more structural elegance. "La secta de los treinta" ("The Sect of the Thirty"), despite its brevity, is another compendium of Borgesiana. In four or five pages are found a mysterious ancient manuscript, a secret society recalling similar groups in "Tlön" or "The Sect of the Phoenix," a discussion of the identity of opposites (Judas and Christ in this case), and a digression on contingency versus necessity. "El disco" ("The Disc") is a somewhat pale reworking of the obsessive object theme, but in an old Norse setting rather than in the Middle Eastern ambience of "El Zahir," ("The Zahir"), Borges's earlier version of the same basic idea.

"Undr" and the collection's title piece, "The Book of Sand," merit closer scrutiny. Both revolve about perennial concerns of Borges: in the first it is the quest for the one word, symbol, or letter that is the key to or the summation of a vast realm; in the second tale it is the notion of infinity as expressed in the infinitely divisible line, or the book of infinite pages. The two ideas—or obsessions—are not unrelated and inform many of Borges's most celebrated canonical texts. "Undr" begins with a highly contrived literary frame built upon a series of embedded narrators. The author reports having seen "these pages" in a publication of a nineteenth-century German scholar who had "unearthed" them from the eleventh-century manuscripts of a certain Adam of Bremen, who in turn states that what he is about to tell was related to him by a traveler from Iceland! The tale itself is laden with Norse atmosphere: the final narrator, a poet, describes his many travels after he learns that "the poetry of the Urns consists of a single word." The abundant details of this quest cannot be fully discussed here, though many of them would be immediately recognizable to readers familiar with the canonical texts. Although the setting is ancient Scandinavia, the mystical quest itself suggests "al-Mu'tasim," the rapidly shifting vagaries of the protagonist's fortune echo the world of "The Lottery in Babylon," and the notion of the single item (in this case a word) that sums up everything recalls "The Aleph." "Undr," nonetheless, has a slightly different twist at its conclusion: a dying bard reveals *the word*, "wonder" ("undr" in old Norse), but the narrator-poet takes up his harp and sings "to a different word." His moribund friend then replies in mysterious, barely audible tones: "You have understood" (*BS*, 87).

"The Book of Sand" begins with a classically crisp Borgesian declaration: "The line is made up of an infinite number of points; the plane of an infinite number of lines; the volume of an infinite number of planes; the hypervolume of an infinite number of volumes" (*BS*, 117). The narrator, in this case an Argentine bibliophile and librarian by profession, is visited by an aged bookseller who offers him a rather bizarre "holy book." The volume, described in some detail, seems to have originated in India; it is tightly printed on very fine paper and its pagination is chaotic. When the narrator tries to find the first page he is completely frustrated: "trying to put my thumb on the fly leaf, I opened the book. It was useless. Every time I tried, a number of pages came between the cover and my thumb. It was as if they kept growing from the book" (*BS*, 119). The narrator—one is tempted to say "Borges," for we have here a very close double—buys the volume and soon becomes obsessed by it. He knows that it has been titled "The Book of Sand" because neither "it nor the sand have any beginning or end" (*BS*, 119). He studies the book, tries to fathom its mystery, suffers insomnia because of it, and finally rids himself of it by hiding the book in an obscure nook of the National Library, where he had formerly worked. He remarks, at the story's conclusion, that the book was "a nightmarish object, an obscene thing that affronted and tainted reality itself" (*BS*, 122). The tale obviously derives from several earlier pieces, but most directly from "The Library of Babel." Unfortunately it seems less successful than its earlier counterpart. Perhaps we have become too familiar with its theme or, more likely, "The Book of Sand," with its somewhat awkward mixing of very real, very mundane elements and an inexplicable unnatural object cannot quite be accepted even metaphorically. For all of Borges's philosophizing, and despite the tale's mysterious trappings, the book itself appears to be some kind of a trick, an artifact from a magician's supply house rather than an effective literary trope.

By the 1980s Borges's vigor as a writer of fiction was clearly waning: the collections just discussed reveal, with a few important exceptions, a growing diminution of his narrative powers. The last book of stories, *Veinticinco de agosto 1983 y otros cuentos*, appeared some three years before his death and, as noted earlier, contains but four tales, only one of which—the title piece—is original. "Utopia of a Tired Man," one of the three previously published pieces, appeared some ten years before in *The Book of Sand* while "La rosa de Paracelso" (The rose of Paracelsus) and "Tigres azules" (Blue tigers) were published together in a thirty-four-page booklet, *Rosa y azul* (Pink and blue, 1977). A few words will suffice for these tales. "La rosa de Paracelso" is set in the workshop of Paracelsus, the sixteenth-century alchemist, where a young disciple or apprentice wishes to see the magical reappearance of a rose after it has been burned. The master does not actually perform the feat until the apprentice leaves, whereupon he takes the ashes in his hand, whispers a word, and the rose, in all its fresh beauty, reappears. Although little else actually happens in the story, there are some interesting discussions between the two regarding faith, credulity, and especially the notion of the creative power of the Word. Like some of the earlier pieces, this text is richer in ideas than in narrative interest.

By contrast, "Tigres azules" is a rather long story set in the Kiplingesque

world of India, with tigers, British colonials, and the like. Its protagonist
and narrator, a Scottish academic, hears that a rare blue tiger is roaming the
hills; he pursues the beast on a "forbidden" plateau, but only finds mysterious blue disks. He collects these seemingly artificial objects and in the balance of the tale he tells how they come to obsess him. For one thing, like the
pages of the book in "The Book of Sand," they can't be counted: they
change number, they resist all calculation. At the story's conclusion he gives
these maddening stones as charity to a passing beggar. Unfortunately, the
tale does not quite hang together. Again like the book of innumerable
pages, the stones seem to be simply fake artifacts; moreover, their relationship to the tigers is forced and unconvincing. Of some interest, nonetheless,
is the fact that Borges's childhood fascination with tigers surfaces once more
and that his long-standing obsession with obsessive objects is again expressed. And, of course, just beneath the surface of the story lies one of
Borges's most fundamental beliefs, namely, that our efforts to make order
out of the universe's chaos are doomed to failure and may indeed drive us
mad.

The book's title piece also takes up a theme that informs a great deal of
Borges's prose and poetry: the notion of himself as "the other." In this tale
Borges, as first-person narrator, is about to register as a guest in an old hotel
in Adrogué, a resort town not far from Buenos Aires and a place much frequented by the Borges family many years ago. He is told that another "J. L.
Borges" has just checked in and is in a room upstairs. He then goes up to
meet a very elderly, infirm double who informs the somewhat "younger"
Borges (who has stated that he had just celebrated his seventy-first birthday) that he is "dreaming" his younger self back in his Buenos Aires home,
and that when his visitor reaches this point in time he will be eighty-four
years old! But the "younger" Borges replies no, that it is *he* who is dreaming
the older man in an Adrogué hotel, at which point the other asks, "Who is
dreaming whom?"[24] In the course of their strange conversation, the younger,
seventy-one-year old Borges reveals that he had committed suicide in the
hotel room; but the eighty-four-year-old Borges appears to refute this by a
cryptic statement: "Therefore I am here." In one of the most interesting ex-
changes between the two, Borges admits that toward the late seventies his
"supposed" work consisted of little more than rough drafts and that he had
finally given up ever writing his "great book." In a tone of playful self-
deprecation he notes that people now speak of a "clumsy" imitator of Borges
who continues to exploit his "museum" of labyrinths, knife fighters, tigers,
bloody battles, long enumerations, "imperfect symmetries that critics excit-
edly discover" along with "not always apocryphal quotations." At this point

he somewhat sadly adds, "This doesn't surprise me. . . . Every writer ends up by being his least intelligent disciple."[25] This comment is, perhaps, a fitting conclusion to the discussion of Borges's very late fiction.

There remain, however, two works of his last decade that must be briefly mentioned. I have said little regarding Borges's essayistic writing of these autumnal years simply because he produced very few texts that might properly be called essays. Some of the short prose pieces in *The Gold of the Tigers* could be considered miniessays as might a few of the prose pieces in *Los conjurados*. However, *Nueve ensayos dantescos* (Nine Dantesque essays, 1982) shows that even in his old age Borges was quite capable of writing clear-cut expository prose. The content and evaluation of these literary essays cannot be taken up here: this task I leave to specialists in the area. In the opening pages of this book I cited a passage from what appears to be Borges's penultimate book: the short, lyrical travel memoirs published late in 1984 as *Atlas*. Given Borges's delight in circularity, in cyclical literary frames, and in philosophies that exploit these notions, it is fitting that our examination of his work close with a few comments on the same text.

In some ways, *Atlas* is a very special item in Borges's total production. While it is essentially a collection of short prose pieces celebrating places visited, it also contains several poems, and is profusely illustrated by photographs. Though Borges signs the prologue and his name appears as the primary author, he notes that the book was done in collaboration with María Kodama. But though there may be some textual evidence of joint authorship, I do not consider it among the genuinely collaborative works.[26] Perhaps the most interesting aspect of the book is that the combination of graphic material and text makes *Atlas* a memorable literary production in the physical sense. In the piece on ballooning, for example, there appears a full-page photo of the ebullient Borges accompanied by Kodama in the basket of a balloon about to ascend. While he expresses the sheer physical joy of the adventure, he seasons the text with his ever present literary references—in this case to Verne and Wells. In another section, on tigers, he fondly recalls a visit to an "Animal World" type of zoological park. Here his friends manage to have a very impressive, full-grown specimen of this beast meet Borges. A photo celebrates the event: a beaming Borges appears, one hand on his cane, the other petting the great Bengal cat: "His tongue licked my face and its indifferent or loving claw lingered atop my head. . . . I will not say that this astonishing tiger . . . is more real than the others . . . but I would like to give thanks here to our friend, that flesh and blood tiger which my senses perceived that morning and whose image comes back to me in the same way as do the images of the Tigers in books."[27] In "Venice," another nicely illustrated piece, we see Borges and Kodama dining in an elegant restaurant or strolling the piazza. My personal reaction to *Atlas* and its photographs is one of gratitude. The thoughts and images of the frail octogenarian who joyfully ventures aloft in a balloon and who finally confronts a real tiger, a creature that for years existed only in his readings of Blake or Kipling, are pleasant ones—they help dispel the image, which Borges himself helped create, that he was even in youth a perennially tired old man. They suggest, by contrast, a rather appealing personality: one characterized by a streak of youthful enthusiasm, of persistent boyishness, and of eternal wonderment.

Chapter Four
The Critical Trajectory

During most of its history Latin American literature has been viewed by the few sophisticated Europeans and North Americans who were even aware of its existence as an interesting manifestation of a picturesque culture: a corpus of writing that either palely reflected Parisian literary fashion or detailed the raw violence of a seething continent. Significant, skillful writers whose work was on the cutting edge of literary innovation, authors who were to shape trends and movements, they believed were not to be found in Mexico, Peru, or Argentina. More often than not, foreigners read the Latin Americans simply for the documentary value of their work rather than for their excellence as creative artists. This same attitude, with certain modifications, was shared by many Latin Americans themselves. Sophisticates of "cosmopolite" leanings—and this would perhaps include the majority of the intellectuals—voraciously consumed foreign literature while they treated homegrown letters with a curious mixture of respect and boredom that amounted to paying their dues to cultural nationalism. This situation has, of course, changed dramatically in recent decades. Nobel prizes have been awarded to several of the hemisphere's major writers; even more important, translations and critical acclaim have brought an entire generation of brilliant Spanish American writers into the international spotlight. The role of Borges in effecting this change was crucial. Stated simply, he was the first Latin American prose writer to be taken seriously by international criticism. How this came about—how Borges emerged from his status as "a mere Argentine," as he was wont to call himself, to that of a world-recognized literary presence—is the main focus of this chapter. A brief consideration of the earliest critical reactions to his work is, however, in order.

Early Polemics

As might be expected, the earliest comments on Borges deal with him primarily as a poet and are almost entirely local in origin. Chiefly minor pieces—reviews of his poetry collections or brief notes—they praise him but seldom attempt any real analysis. By the early thirties, however, Borges was becoming important enough to receive more serious criticism; and in 1933 the Buenos Aires magazine *Megáfono,* recognizing his growing stature, conducted an opinion poll on the rising young author. Some fifteen contributors participated, including several men who are now counted among the most distinguished writers and critics of the Hispanic world: Amado Alonso, Eduardo Mallea, Ulises Petit de Murat, and Enrique Anderson Imbert. By this time Borges's essays had attracted almost as much attention as his poetry; as a result, the *Megáfono* writers begin to differentiate Borges the poet from Borges the prose writer. Anderson Imbert, for example, attacks Borges as a critic and essayist, though he admits that his verse is probably more praiseworthy. Leon Ostrov noted that the two activities—that of poet and critical essayist—were mutually self-destructive.

Borges's early reservations about writing fiction seem to have had some foundation. At least so it seemed when the jury charged with the task of selecting the winner of the National Literary Prize for the year 1941 rejected his first collection of stories, *The Garden of Forking Paths.* A host of writers and critics, especially those of his own generation, rallied round their defeated comrade in a remarkable show of solidarity. Their outrage found expression in the pages of *Sur,* at the time only a decade old but well on its way to becoming one of the Hispanic world's truly great literary magazines. Borges's close friend and collaborator, Adolfo Bioy Casares, was as cutting as anyone in his assessment of the situation: "The commission . . . awarded the two first prizes to persons whom no one could confuse with writers." Eduardo Mallea, the rising novelist of the generation, was especially eloquent in his praise, comparing Borges's prose to that of Domingo Faustino Sarmiento. Luis E. Soto emphasized Borges's essential *criollismo,* while the highly respected Dominican critic Pedro Henríquez Ureña underscored Borges's originality in what has become a famous statement: "There may be those who think that Borges is original because he proposes to be. I think quite the contrary: Borges would be original even when he might propose not to be." And Amado Alonso, in describing Borges's literary language, coined a phrase as memorable as it is untranslatable: "un estilo tan estilo" ("a style so style"). Although all the contributors seemed to agree that the award should have gone to Borges, a few indicated that their support was not unqualified.

The reservations of several vociferous compatriots surfaced even more dramatically a few years later. When Borges published his second collection of prose pieces, his celebrated *Ficciones* (1944), Ernesto Sábato, a "committed" writer of Sartrean leanings and an author of considerable reputation, wrote a sharply critical review of the book in the prestigious review *Sur.* The ideas expressed in this piece have since become classical statements of the anti-Borges position. Sábato first attacks Borges's overt use of literary sources for his fiction: he dismisses these as "underlying fossils." He then points out Borges's tendency to reshuffle the same limited number of ideas—a literary trait that was apparent even as early as 1945: "The influence that Borges has kept on having on Borges seems insuperable. Will he be condemned from now on to plagiarize himself?" Borges's lack of seriousness also irritated Sábato. Two points that he makes in this regard are probably true: that Borges's fantasies do not have the nightmarish involvement found in Kafka and that Borges's interest in theological matters is merely "a game of a nonbeliever." Sábato also attacks Borges's overall views on fiction: his fondness for the "geometrization" of narrative and his critique of the psychological novel. Yet, like a number of others who have reservations about Borges's prose, Sábato expresses considerable respect for his poetry, and thus he concludes his article with a rich statement that sums up the ambivalence in his attitude: "I see you, Borges, above all as a Great Poet. And afterward, thus: arbitrary, brilliant, tender, a watchmaker, great, triumphant, daring, timid, a failure, magnificent, unhappy, limited, infantile, and immortal."[1]

It is ironic that the first book-length study devoted to Borges should have been essentially negative. Adolfo Prieto, a young Argentine critic, in his *Borges y la nueva generación* (1954), spoke for a different generation with a radically different concept of the relationship between writers and the world. "Borges is a writer for the writers of *his* generation" is the leitmotiv running through Prieto's study. The younger men of letters, he claims, can't even "react against" Borges. One of the clearest statements of his opinion appears early in his book: "Detective fiction and fantasy suffer from the same defects . . . as the novel of chivalry and the pastoral novel. These defects spring basically from the complete gratuity of these genres, from their absolute forgetting of man, from their schematization of reality."[2] Even as a writer of fantasy, Borges is found lacking. Prieto concentrates his attack on the story "The Aleph," a tale well spiced with Borgesian humor though one that might seem rather inept if taken with complete seriousness. As might be expected, Prieto does exactly this. He objects most of all to what he calls "the direct presentation" of the fantastic. He feels that Borges fails in not preparing the reader for the series of "ineffable" events that follow once the author descends into Carlos Argentino's basement. "Everything is possible in the world of fantasy, provided we are captured by it. . . . If our feet remain on the ground, the attempt fails. . . . The most difficult task . . . for the acutely imaginative artist is to transform the earthbound spectator into a fantastic spectator, to stamp his passport to a world different from our[s]

. . . . The realm of the fantastic, viewed from the outside . . . is simply absurd."[3] Prieto's objections, taken in the general sense, are justified. Their application to "The Aleph" however, is not—unless we, like the critic, assume a dead seriousness that the tale lacks.

Though the views of Sábato and Prieto represent positions that have persisted up to the present, they could not prevail against the general acclaim that has grown steadily since the late forties and early fifties. In addition to an ever-increasing stream of laudatory critical notices, Borges could find consolation in having his *Ficciones* awarded the 1944 "Prize of Honor" of the Argentine Writers Association and in finally winning the National Prize for Literature for his 1952 collection of essays, *Other Inquisitions*. Several more balanced, more appreciative, books on Borges's work soon appeared: Ríos Patrón's *Jorge Luis Borges* (1955), Tamayo and Ruíz Díaz's *Borges enigma y clave* (1955), and Fernández Moreno's *Esquema de Borges* (1957).

Perhaps the first really scholarly exegesis of Borges's main themes also appeared in 1957. Ana María Barrenechea's *La expresión de la irrealidad en la obra de Jorge Luis Borges* (translated under the title *Borges the Labyrinth Maker*) is the culmination of several years' work. The author, Argentine by nationality but educated in the United States, published the book in Mexico. The study, as its title suggests, is limited to the notion of "irreality," especially in Borges's prose fiction. The author states clearly in her conclusion that this is only one of many aspects of his writings, and to interpret him solely on the basis of his cultivation of "irreality" might lead to "a purely negative and false idea" of Borges's work. Barrenechea's fundamental attitude toward Borges is one of great admiration, though she does not attempt to write literary propaganda in his behalf. Although this book gets close to some of the most basic concerns of Borges, it may err on the side of seriousness: one finds in Barrenechea's work little appreciation for Borgesian irony and high humor. Note, for example, the following: "To undermine the reader's belief in the concreteness of life, Borges attacks those fundamental concepts on which the security of living itself is founded: the universe, personality, and time. The universe is converted into a meaningless chaos abandoned to chance or ruled by inhuman gods."[4] Or, from Barrenechea's concluding statements: "Borges is an admirable writer pledged to destroy reality and convert Man into a shadow. The process of dissolution of concepts on which Man's belief in the concreteness of his life is founded . . . has been analyzed. Also viewed here have been the anguishing presence of the Infinite and the disintegration of the substantial."[5] In historical perspective, however, *La expresión de la irrealidad en la obra de Jorge Luis Borges* is clearly one of the most significant studies to have appeared—and doubly so, in that Robert Lima's excellent 1965 translation of the book was instrumental in making Borges better known to readers of English.

An International Celebrity

The critical acclaim that he was soon to enjoy cannot be fully appreciated without considering certain events in Borges's life. One of these, his fortuitous contact with a group of French writers and critics, had an incalculable effect on his career. This group had taken refuge in Buenos Aires during World War II. With the help of Borges's friend, Victoria Ocampo, the director of the review *Sur,* they even established a French literary journal in Argentina. One of the most important figures among them, Roger Caillois, became a close friend of Borges. Through his efforts and those of others, Borges's work began appearing in translation as early as 1951. By the end of the decade the prestigious Gallimard publishing house had made virtually all his major prose writings available to French readers.[6] Finally, in 1961, Borges shared the international Prix Formentor with Samuel Beckett. This award, sponsored by a consortium of six publishers representing six major Western countries, provided for the translation and publication of *Ficciones* in each nation. This important recognition was followed by invitations to teach or to lecture at major universities on both sides of the Atlantic. His hitherto uneventful life was now punctuated by travel, the receipt of honorary degrees, and the granting of interviews. In short, by the mid-1960s Borges had become an international literary celebrity.

Critical comment on his work immediately reflected his newly acquired status. Interest in Borges within the English-speaking world began early among specialists in Spanish American literature, but with the appearance of translations in the early sixties a growing appreciation of him became evident beyond academia. Paul de Man, writing for the sophisticated audience of the *New York Review of Books* late in 1964, stressed the literary "duplicity," irony, and even sinister overtones of this "complex" new writer whom he called "a modern master."[7] Published about a year later, John Updike's essay in the *New Yorker* can be considered a milestone in the American understanding of the Argentine writer. Updike's long article is candid, witty, and full of relevancy for the North American reader. He is especially sensitive to the problems posed by the "arrival" of a previously unknown foreign writer on the international or, in this case, American literary scene. What is most interesting is that Updike sees a real possibility that such a writer may have an important effect on our literature. "The question is, I think, whether or not Borges's lifework . . . can serve, in its gravely considered

oddity, as any kind of clue to the way out of the dead-end narcissism and
downright trashiness of present American fiction."[8] Perhaps what appeals
most to the reviewer is the fact that "Borges's narrative innovations spring
from a clear sense of technical crisis. For all his modesty . . . he proposes
some sort of essential revision in literature itself."[9] Yet Updike concludes his
introductory observations by remarking that Borges "seems to be the man
for whom literature has no future," a casual statement that may well be an
important clue to Borges's current vogue. Throughout his article, Updike
hits the mark. He sees the essential differences between Borges and Kafka
with great clarity; his interpretations of the Borgesian attitudes toward eroticism and "femaleness" are well taken; finally, his summation of Borges's
thoughts on the novel is especially penetrating: "Certainly the traditional
novel as a transparent imitation of human circumstances has 'a distracted or
tired air.' Ironic and blasphemous as Borges's hidden message may seem,
the texture and method of his creations . . . answer to a deep need in contemporary literary art—the need to confess the fact of artifice."[10]

The American novelist John Barth is another writer who has expressed a
great attraction for Borges's fiction. In a provocative article, "The Literature
of Exhaustion" (1967), Barth observes the state of the arts and clearly is disturbed by what he sees. Like Updike, he views contemporary art as having
reached a dead end, or a point of no return. Pop art, "happenings," the
"intermedia" arts, and the like have at their roots a "tendency to eliminate
not only the traditional audience . . . but also the most traditional notion of
the artist: the Aristotelian conscious agent who achieves with technique and
cunning the artistic effect; in other words, one endowed with uncommon
talent, who has moreover developed and disciplined that endowment into
virtuosity."[11] Barth's ideas on contemporaneity in art form the next basic
step in his argument. It is essential, he feels, for a good literary work to be
"technically up-to-date": "A good many current novelists write turn-of-the-
century-type novels, only in more or less mid-twentieth-century language
and about contemporary people and topics: this makes them considerably
less interesting (to me) than excellent writers who are also technically contemporary: Joyce and Kafka, for instance, in their time, and in ours, Samuel
Beckett and Jorge Luis Borges."[12] One of the hallmarks of our time, Barth
goes on to say, is the fact that a sense of "ultimacies" pervades everything
from theology to weaponry. Borges, he notes, is not only *aware* of a esthetic
ultimacies, but *uses* them in his literature. This notion is further underscored in Barth's discussion of "Tlön, Uqbar, Orbis Tertius," and again in
his analysis of Borges's fascination with the *regressus in infinitum*—"an
image of the exhaustion, or attempted exhaustion, of possibilities." For the

"exhaustion of possibilities, like the "felt ultimacies" in contemporary life, leads toward an "intellectual dead-end." Barth relates Borges's ideas on the impossibility (or at least the difficulty) of originality in literature to the same theme, that is, to the "used-upness of certain forms or exhaustion of certain possibilities."[13]

It was in France, however, that Borges's literary stock had its earliest and most dramatic rise. That the French had begun translating his work in the 1950s has already been noted. The critical response to this very different kind of Latin American writer was lively and intense. Sylvia Molloy records some fifty items of French criticism dealing with Borges during the decade. The same observer also notes that by the late fifties and early sixties the adjective *borgésien* had become a commonplace in Parisian literary circles, and that a frequently heard question among the literati was "Avez-vous lu Borges?"[14] In addition to his winning the Formentor Prize, Borges's position as "a point of reference"—to quote Molloy again—for French critics was further enhanced by a discussion of him in the influential literary journal *Tel Quel* in the autumn of 1962 and by the publication in 1964 of a voluminous special issue of the review *L'Herne* dedicated to him. The latter event is especially significant because the review included comments on his work by an impressive array of critics representing the Americas, Germany, Spain, and of course many of France's leading literary lights—Valéry Larbaud, Jean Ricardou, Claude Ollier, Jean Wahl, and Gérard Genette.

The sheer volume of critical studies, scholarly essays, reviews, bibliographic works, and informal observations that have appeared in the quarter century since this "internationalization" of Borges is almost overwhelming. A stream of solid critical work has continued to flow from North American publishers, both within and outside academia; the Hispanic world has also maintained steady interest in him, as have the French and English, not to mention commentators in such distant places as Bucharest, Oslo, or Tokyo. Obviously it is impossible to discuss all, or even a representative sampling, of this critical reaction within the limits of this study. However, I will mention a few of the more important—and more accessible—items, and then explore Borges's relationship to certain major critical and literary trends.

Following the essays on Borges by Updike, de Man, and Barth, the first book-length studies in English appeared: Ronald Christ's *The Narrow Act: Borges' Art of Allusion* (1969) and Carter Wheelock's provocative analysis of Borgesian symbolism, *The Mythmaker: A Study of Motif and Symbol in the Short Stories of Jorge Luis Borges* (1969). A bit earlier, several basic investigations had been published in Spanish: Zunilda Gertel's *Borges y su retorno a la poesía* (1967); Guillermo Sucre's *Borges el poeta* (1967); and

Jaime Alazraki's fundamental study, *La prosa narrativa de Jorge Luis Borges* (1968). To these may be added several broad-scoped works published by authors intent on making Borges better known among general readers. Often, these volumes were part of a university or a commercial press "author" series such as my earlier study of Borges (1970), Alazraki (1971, Columbia Essays on Modern Writers), and Cohen (1974, Barnes & Noble "Modern Writers" series). Another facet of the interest in Borges was the continued appearance of numerous interviews, dialogues, and "conversations" with him. While not really opening new critical perspectives, these have on occasion offered the student of Borges interesting personal tidbits or insights into his literary art. Typical of these publications are those of Burgin (1969), Sorrentino (1973), Vázquez (1977), and Guibert's extensive chapter on Borges in her widely read volume *Seven Voices* (1973).

The biographical perspective also dominates Emir Rodríquez Monegal's lengthy, detailed, and often surprising volume, *Jorge Luis Borges: A Literary Biography* (1978). Considering the contemporary critical climate, any work that emphasizes biographical determinants and elements may be viewed with some suspicion, especially in the case of a writer whose life—at least outwardly—has been remarkably uneventful. Thus opinions vary as to how well the author has met the challenge of producing a "literary biography" of Borges. For John Sturrock, writing in the *New York Times,* the book "has the virtues of a workmanlike chronicle, but none of the charms of mature biography." The same commentator accuses Rodríquez Monegal of doing a "terrible thing" in his "grubbing around" for the roots of Borges's fiction in the dull details of the writer's prosaic life. By contrast, V. S. Pritchett in the *New Yorker* considered Rodríguez Monegal's book "an absorbing, even exciting work of discreet detection, written with verve, often very moving."

These seemingly disparate assessments, however, do give a fair idea of what *Jorge Luis Borges: A Literary Biography* is all about. Moreover, they underscore a basic problem inherent in the genre itself. Granted there is value in knowing that the rambling old hotel at Adrogué and the dreary municipal library provided the physical settings for certain stories; that Borges's by-now-famous 1938 accident and hospitalization inspired "The South"; or that the "Maurice Abramowicz" who appears as an erudite commentator in a footnote to "Three Versions of Judas" was in fact an old schoolmate from Geneva. Yet some may wonder why all this merits such painstaking attention. Don't all authors rely upon bits and pieces of their personal experience, places they have visited and people they have known, to supply raw material for their fictional creations? However, it may be well to remind those who intone the credo of contemporary textual criticism that there is in fact some very real "reality" behind the printed pages of Borges's texts. Leaving aside literary biography's values or limitations, what can be said of this specific example of the genre? On balance, the work is a useful, intelligently presented compendium of what Rodríquez Monegal—and a number of other critics, friends, and interviewers—have been able to piece together of Borges's life and of how that life has entered into his works. Much of the material is already familiar to students of Argentina's most celebrated writer, but the author does add new information, clarifies details of what had been sketchy areas, and, when hard biographical data are lacking, offers some intriguing speculations.

A number of provocative comparative studies have made important contributions to Borges scholarship in recent years. Questions of influences, affinities, and parallels are discussed in such studies as Stark's *The Literature of Exhaustion: Borges, Nabokov and Barth* (1974), Sosnowski's *Borges y la cabala* (1976), Covizzi's *O insólito em Guimarães Rosa e Borges* (1978), as well as in a large number of doctoral dissertations dealing with possible relationships between Borges and a host of other writers (Beckett, Hawthorne, Poe, Cortázar, Sarduy, and Pynchon, for example).

Perhaps the most fascinating study of this type is J. D. Crossan's *Raid on the Articulate: Comic Eschatology in Jesus and Borges* (1976), because it illustrates just how far the matter of affinities and literary analogies can be pushed. A critical tour de force, Crossan's essay is based on the notion that there is a kind of parallelism in the iconoclasm of both Jesus and Borges. For the Argentine writer, the essence of this iconoclasm lies in his "comic subversion on one giant and central aspect of our literary heritage, the tradition of the Book. And especially on its most fascinating example, the Realistic Novel."[15] For Jesus, a similar relationship exists with reference to the legalistic Judaic tradition, or what Crossan calls the Nazarene's deliberate comic subversion of "the wise and prudent necessity of . . . law." The ends toward which the two direct their iconoclasm or "comic subversion" " are very different, being literary in one case and religious in the other. Crossan supports his argument by abundant examples from Scripture and from Borges's writings: he captivates his reader by a freewheeling, flamboyant, yet intellectual style and by rich citations from a host of other writers, among whom contemporary French critics figure prominently. In addition, he is obviously on familiar terms with biblical scholarship (he is a professor of theology at DePauw) as well as with current works on Borges.

Yet, despite the well-wrought argument, the impressive scholarship, and the appropriately turned phrase, there is something strangely gratuitous about Crossan's essay. That both Jesus and Borges are iconoclasts and employ "comic subversion" may be true, but it is debatable whether this formal relationship justifies their being considered in a single study. Although Crossan does not suggest that we view Borges as a great religious teacher or that we think of Jesus as a brilliant innovative litterateur, the juxtaposition of the names in the book's title could easily lead the casual observer to assume that such substantive similarities do exist. The true devotee of Borges will nonetheless find Crossan's volume fascinating and will not be deterred by the thought that it may be gratuitous. After all, Borgesian gamesmanship is infectious. Wasn't it Menard himself who wrote a technical study "proposing, discussing, and finally rejecting" the notion that the game of chess might be enriched by the elimination of the rook's pawn?

Throughout the eighties critics and scholars have continued to probe and organize the rich corpus of Borgesian writings. Gene Bell-Villada, for example, published his *Borges and His Fiction: A Guide to His Mind and Art* (1981), an ambitious overview in which the author attempts—with considerable success—to survey Borges's work in terms of literary politics, critical trends, and the like. Scholarly effort of a more technical sort may be seen in two other recent publications: Daniel Balderston's invaluable vade mecum for any Borgephile, *The Literary Universe of Jorge Luis Borges* (1986), whose subtitle, *An Index of References and Allusions to Persons, Titles, and Places in His Writings,* gives a good idea of its scope, and David W. Foster's *Jorge Luis Borges: An Annotated Primary and Secondary Bibliography* (1984), certainly the most complete Borges bibliography to have appeared.

The Detractors

The negative assessment of Borges's work has, as we have seen, its roots in the early polemics of the thirties and forties. Intelligently formulated criticism of this kind can often illuminate basic questions regarding a writer's literary tenets as well as issues dealing with the place of art in the broader context of society or politics. Of course, much of this negative criticism has not been intelligently formulated or objective. One suspects that a good deal of it derives either from gross misunderstanding of Borges or simply from envy. At any rate, by the mid-1940s and early 1950s, after Borges had published many of his major prose fictions, the tone of his detractors had changed. Sábato was one of the earliest to lead this attack. A highly politicized younger generation of writers, demanding "commitment" of themselves and of their mentors, soon followed. A work that well illustrates this phase of the negative criticism is Prieto's previously mentioned *Borges y la nueva generación:* the mood of Prieto and others like him is nicely clarified by E. Rodríguez Monegal in his study of the period, *El juicio de los parricidas* (1956).

What seems to underlie the views of those who took issue with Borges is in essence the familiar polemic between the defender of art for art's sake and those who hold to the idea that writers must, in some manner, express political or at least philosophical commitment in their literary creations. Thus, even when he is attacked for his "geometrical" narratives, his "mathematical plots," or his stylistic quirks, it is often this issue that illicits the criticism. Sábato's comments—of 1963 in this case, though they had changed little since his previously cited review of *Ficciones*—illustrate the problem well: "The so-called theology of Borges is the game of a nonbeliever and the subject matter of his effete literature. There is, in the depths of his being, a horror of flesh and blood life. . . . He takes refuge in his tower and there like a pure mathematician . . . he devotes himself to his Leibnitzian games. (With a clear conscience, without nostalgia, without sadness, without any sense of guilt or of frustration?)"[16] In short, Sábato, like many others, demands of Borges or any writer dedication, faith, passion, or commitment to something beyond his literary creation. Other Argentine writers of the fifties are a good deal less thoughtful in their deprecation of Borges. Attacking from various vantage points—Peronist, traditional nationalist, or heterodox Marxist—critics like Jorge Abelardo Ramos in his *Crisis y resurrección de la literatura argentina* (1954) or J. J. Hernández Arregui in his *Imperialismo y cultura* (1957) hardly discuss literary matters but simply consider Borges an outcast because in their view he had not contributed to a "national" literature or because he symbolized the cosmopolite taste of a small circle of Buenos Aires intellectuals.

The bulk of the negative criticism of Borges has been and still is Argentine in origin. However, on relatively rare occasions, non-Argentine writers have expressed strong reservations regarding his work. Often their reactions stem from their rejection of his moderate—some would say conservative—political views, or from the fact that his critics hold to an essentially different concept of the relationship between literature and reality. Or, as noted earlier, simple envy or misunderstanding may account for their attitude. One wonders, for example, which of these factors prompted the Spanish novelist and Nobel laureate Camilo José Cela to write the following in a 1953 magazine article: "Jorge Luis Borges is a phantom, he is the great *bluff* of Argentine literature. At times an unsophisticated young lady may perhaps find his stories acceptable. Jorge Luis Borges is a hybrid product without any great interest."[17]

Latin American politics of recent decades are unquestionably closely re-

lated to the trajectory of the negative criticism of Borges. For one thing,
Havana, which by the early sixties had become a literary center for the continent's Marxist intellectuals, provided a new locus from which Borges
could be attacked. Not that the Cubans wrote a great deal about him; indeed, their tendency to ignore him while lauding other important Latin
American writers seems to have been quite deliberate. Of this limited
Cuban comment, the observations of Roberto Fernández Retamar, one of
the top intellectuals in the Castro regime, should be noted, Writing in his
essay *Calibán: apuntes sobre la cultura de nuestra América* (1973), he echoes
much Argentine criticism by attacking Borges for his European orientation
and lack of sympathy for the lower classes. Such publications as the
Castrista journal *Casa de las Américas* on occasion gave Borges's detractors a
prestigious forum, of broad circulation, in which they could criticize him.
Some of Sábato's comments on Borges appeared in the journal, as well as an
especially perceptive critique by another Argentine writer, Noé Jitrik.

    Jitrik's essay "Estructura y significado en *Ficciones* de Jorge Luis Borges"
(1969) merits special attention because it represents one of the most intelligently conceived critiques to have been written. For one thing, Jitrik pro-
ceeds analytically from Borges's texts. Early in his essay, after discussing
several key *ficciones,* he pinpoints a remark by the writer-protagonist of "El
milagro secreto": "Hladik favored verse, because it prevents the audience
from forgetting unreality, which is essential to art." Jitrik goes on to deduce
that this indicates that Borges is affirming "a certain theory of art whose pa-
rameters might be unreality, fictional invention and above all the distinction
between what is explicit (the anecdote) and what is hidden within the structure of that which is explicit."[18] Moreover, Jitrik holds, such hints as these in
Borges's texts indicate a critical approach that most commentators have not
really followed.

    It would be impossible to trace the full development of Jitrik's argument
in this study. It is sufficient to note that toward the end of his essay he established a kind of dialectic between "action" and "thought" that he feels characterizes mainstream Argentine letters. Yet Borges and those like him do
not really conceive of "thought" as a stimulus to "action." Jitrik thus concludes his essay with the following observation: "Clearly this conflict should
be explained throughout the course of Argentine literature in order to relate
Borges to it. It is sufficient to say at this point that Borges demonstrates it in
all its splendor and in its true form: he is, above all else, an Argentine intellectual for whom the frozen universality of thought can perfectly stifle the
transforming function of thought."[19]

    Not all of the negative criticism of Borges is as intelligent as the example just cited. Indeed, some of it consists of sheer personal vituperation or simply questionable, idiosyncratic comment. A relatively obscure pamphlet like Alfredo Arfini's *Borges: pobre ciego balbuciente* (1968) is an example of the former, whereas Blas Matomoro's heavy-handed putdown, *Jorge Luis Borges o el juego trascendente* (1971), might typify the latter. Finally, various aspects of the anti-Borges position have been studied and organized in a helpful anthology of negative criticism, Juan Fló's *Contra Borges* (1978). Although this volume could hardly include everything written on the subject, Fló's balanced assessment of the negative position more than compensates for any omissions: in short, the book is to be recommended as a most convenient source of material on Borges's detractors.

Borges and the New Criticism: A Symbiosis

Borges's provocative and oft-quoted observation that "every writer creates his precursors" could, with slight modification, be applied to the relationship between authors and critics. Though "every writer creates his critics" may be an overly schematic statement, there is some evidence that the work of genuinely great literary creators has often required critics to reshape the existing theoretical apparatus or to develop entirely new positions. This process has particular relevance with respect to the critical reception of Borges's work.

That a major shift—one might even say revolution—in critical theory took place in the mid-twentieth century can hardly be questioned. The diffusion of structuralist, poststructuralist, and related critical approaches that emanated from Paris during the fifties and early sixties coincides with, or follows shortly after, several important purely literary phenomena: the French *nouveau roman,* the Latin American "new narrative," and, of course, the publication and translation of Borges's canonical texts. While critics like Blanchot, Barthes, Genette, Todorov, and their successors examined an extensive literary corpus—including much writing of the distant past—one wonders if their innovative theoretical approaches would have emerged if not for modernists like Joyce, Woolf, or Kafka and, more important, if not for the aesthetic ambience created by such problematic writers as Beckett, Pynchon, Robbe-Grillet, and Jorge Luis Borges. To prove or disprove this intriguing idea is not only difficult, but obviously lies beyond the limits of this study. Nonetheless, it can be shown that several of the new critics read Borges and drew considerably from his fiction and essays in developing their own theoretical positions. Given this situation, it is not surprising that a good deal of the more recent critical work on Borges should, in a sense, close the cycle by adopting structuralist and/or poststructuralist approaches to his texts. Thus, under the spell of the French critical circle—and its branch offices in places like Buenos Aires or New Haven—scholars could reexamine Borges's work and discover textual riches which earlier, less sophisticated critics, either overlooked or misinterpreted.

The simple fact that Borges's creative writing as well as his critical notions show an affinity for structuralist thinking is, in my view, irrefutable. His highly structured "geometric" narratives and his underlying concept of literature (as well as language) as an arbitrary system of ordering an essentially chaotic world coincide remarkably with the fundamental concepts of structuralism. Note, for example, a typical description of this movement as given by Peter Caws in the *Dictionary of the History of Ideas:* "The basic tenet of structuralism on the substantive level might be rendered as follows: what makes anything intelligible to man is a coincidence of structure between it and him. Nature is not intelligible except insofar as we are able to formulate its workings in theories of our own construction."[20] Of course, Borges did not read or comment upon contemporary structuralism, though his general interest in language, in earlier movements such as nominalism or in the thought of John Wilkins, indicate a high degree of intellectual kinship. And finally, he expressed only ingenuous amusement when informed that some of the new French critical theorists found that his texts "enriched" their work.[21]

This attitude notwithstanding, there are definite links between Borges's writing and the new criticism. Emir Rodríguez Monegal, in an important essay of 1972, showed how such major theoreticians as Maurice Blanchot, Jean Ricardou, and especially Gérard Genette incorporated, despite some misreadings, Borgesian ideas into their critical systems. Others have also seen the relationship between Borges and structuralist poetics. David Foster, writing in 1973, observed: "that Borges's fiction had for so long before the critically conscious moment of the sixties attracted such interest for its apparently total rupture with established literary values and principles explains to a great degree how we can see him as having sensed, *avant la lettre,* the esthetic potential of structuralist principles."[22] Even beyond the first wave of structuralism—the *Tel Quel* group and the activity of the fifties and early sixties—there are some fascinating relationships between Borges and other writers on the fringe of or beyond the movement.

One of the very first French theorists to show an affinity for Borges was the philosopher and critic Maurice Blanchot, a kind of link between the older generation and the younger structuralists. In one of his most celebrated works, *Le Livre à venir* (1959), he notes Borges's rendering of the infinite—as expressed in "The Aleph"—as being especially fruitful; he also explores the rich possibilities of Borges's notion of the Book as the Universe. Rodríguez Monegal suggests that Blanchot's use of these ideas is quite early, even antedating the publication of *Le Livre à venir* by several years.[23] Genette first reveals the influence of Borges in his 1964 contribution to the special issue of *L'Herne:* his essay "La littérature selon Borges" reappeared two years later, slightly modified and under a different title, as a chapter in his basic work on narrative, *Figures* (1966). Genette discusses several Borgesian texts that revolve about the idea of authorship and influences, but he seems to focus upon Borges's underlying notion of the identity of all books and all authors. There are other passages in *Figures* that further illustrate Genette's debt to the Argentine. In the key chapter "Structuralism et critique littéraire" the French critic analyzes the subtle interplay between the reader's sense of "expectation" and the "surprise" revealed by the author. To emphasize the importance of this process, this "efficatiousness" of literature, he cites Borges's comment that "the great poet. . . is he who reveals rather than invents."[24] And, like many others, Genette seems fascinated by Menard's *Quijote:* in a discussion of Shakespeare he notes that when we read the dramatist we see him from the viewpoint of the contemporaries of Brecht and Claudel, just as the modern Cervantes is a contemporary of Kafka. He then cites Borges's observation that if we could know how any single page of today's writing would be read in the year 2000, we would be able to know the literature of the next century.[25] Several other references to Borges are found in *Figures,* giving further evidence of Genette's close reading of his texts.

It is debatable whether or not Michel Foucault was a genuine literary critic; similarly his status as a structuralist may also be questioned. It is clear, however, that since the mid-1960s Foucault's brilliant and complex ruminations on the nature of language, social institutions, and literature have had a substantial impact on contemporary thought. If we take his statement at face value—always a bit dangerous in the case of sophisticates given to irony—his debt to Borges is tremendous: the first line of his crucial work *The Order of Things* (1966) reads, "This book first arose out of a passage in Borges, out of the laughter that shattered, as I read the passage, all the familiar landmarks of my thought."[26] The specific text to which Foucault refers is the essay on "The Analytic Language of John Wilkins."[27] In it, Borges describes "a certain Chinese encyclopedia" whose thoroughly outlandish classification of animals defies all the usual conventions of taxonomy. There we find categories such as "those belonging to the Emperor," "embalmed," "sucking pigs," "fabulous," "those included in the present classification," "those drawn with a fine camelhair brush," "stray dogs," "those that from a long way off look like flies," and so on. Foucault moves from a consideration of this bizarre scheme to his own idea of "heterotopia"—the nonplace of language—as the only realm where all these strange creatures might meet.[28] The implications of this idea, especially as they bear upon language and reality, are obviously great: how Foucault develops them is, of necessity, far beyond the scope of this study. But before leaving Foucault it should be noted that the text just cited is not the only example of the French thinker's recourse to Borges. In the English-language anthology of his essays, *Language, Counter-Memory, Practice* (1977), he again chooses a Borgesian epigraph—the celebrated remark that "every writer creates his precursors." Later on he makes several additional references to the Argentine master, as in his essay "Language to Infinity," where he examines "The Secret Miracle" in the context of his discussion of metafiction, of "language . . . that tells of itself."[29]

It is more difficult to find overt linkages between Borges's poetics (as articulated in his essays and suggested by his fiction) and the critical tenets of Kristeva, Todorov, or Derrida. Yet certain parallelisms clearly exist. Borges's masterful use of intertextual references is one that comes to mind immediately in connection with Kristeva; his penchant for embedding or "opening" his narrative with unresolved, embryonic alternate plots parallels some of Todorov's ideas on narratology,[30] and his playful manipulation of alternate or "added" worlds—Tlön and Uqbar, for example— suggests the corrosion of the logocentric realm of Western discourse, a motif associated with Derrida. In fact, the Borges-Derrida relationship may be quite tenable, as Roberto González Echeverría has pointed out in a thought-provoking article first published in 1983.[31] Citing Derrida's use of two Borgesian epigraphs (one from "The Fearful Sphere of Pascal" and the other from "Tlön, Uqbar, Orbis Tertius") in his essay "Plato's Pharmacy," González develops a finespun thesis on the points of contact between the two writers and their significance for Latin American letters. Again, to pursue his line of thought—one that leaves more questions unanswered than resolved—would take us far afield.

Although the precise nature and extent of Borges's influence on contemporary literary theory may be difficult to determine, in my view there is little doubt that it does exist. There is even less doubt that scholars have found it profitable to apply structuralist and poststructuralist analysis to his works. In fact, since about 1970 some of the most interesting studies have been based on these new approaches. We have already seen some evidence of this trend in Crossan's *Raid on the Articulate* and in Jitrik's piece on structure in

Ficciones. Two additional volumes merit individual attention in this regard: British critic John Sturrock's *Paper Tigers: The Ideal Fictions of Jorge Luis Borges* (1977) and Sylvia Molloy's *Las letras de Borges* (1979). The first of these focuses chiefly on the stories of *Ficciones* and *The Aleph*, texts that in Sturrock's view "set the student of Borges the most, and the right, questions." He also holds that a careful analysis of this corpus of work leads not only to an explication of a particular author but also to "larger questions in the so-called theory of Fiction." Sturrock's interest, throughout his well-wrought study, is extremely textual, extremely internal: while he is not an orthodox follower of a narrowly defined school, his debt to contemporary criticism, especially to Barthes, is clear. His remarks in the book's final chapter, "The Uses of Uselessness," touch upon a point that lies at the center of the continuing discussion of Borges's ultimate worth as a writer. Quoting Pierre Menard, Sturrock observes, "There is no intellectual exercise that is not, in the end, useless." He then goes on to state that "there may be something very old-fashioned, and Art-for-Art's-Sake-ish, about a defense of literature which claims that literature is valuable precisely *because* it is useless."[32] He also perceptively notes that a justification of literary activity on these grounds will probably seem "more challenging" to Argentine readers.

Like her British colleague, Molloy approaches Borges well provided with the instruments of contemporary criticism. Also like Sturrock, Molloy has her structuralism and semiotics well digested: her method indicates that she can use traditional criticism as well as the insights of a Derrida, a Genette, or a Todorov—writers with whom she has obviously had a long-standing familiarity. It is difficult to generalize about a work so laden with penetrating observations as *Las letras de Borges.* However, one idea appears to dominate the study: Molloy holds that the formal aspects of Borges's texts—his syntax, his erasures and *disjecta membra,* his enumerations and often bizarre taxonomies, in short, the total textual morphology—has a message, a significance that is more important than his more obvious "themes" or "content." Among the finest pages of her study are those in which she analyzes the way that Borges emphasizes and personalizes *el gesto,* her section on "the pleasures of interpolation," and the perceptive discussion on intra- and intertextual references.

It would not be possible to discuss here the many individual studies and articles on Borges that employ, in varying degrees, structuralist, semiotic, or poststructuralist approaches. However, by way of example, two studies— both exploring the same story, "The Garden of the Forking Paths"—may

serve to illustrate how contemporary criticism can breathe new life into frequently discussed canonical texts.

Stephen Rudy's "The Garden *of* and *in* Borges's 'Garden of the Forking
Paths' " (1980) takes as its point of departure Michel Foucault's observation that Borges's language often creates a "heterotopia," defined as "an impossible and frightening non-place." Rudy holds that "what Foucault finds
Borges doing with words in general we find the same writer doing with
plots in 'The Garden of the Forking Paths.' "[33] Plot, for Rudy, can be "a
central symbolic element embodying the author's subversive metaphysics,"
as much as thematics or imagery. To set up his analysis he divides the plot
into four elements: (a) the frame, (b) the detective plot, (c) the metaphysical
mystery Plot, and (d) the crossing of the plots. Rudy maintains that the apparently historical, factual framing device is altered and made ambiguous to
such an extent that "it is there for the purpose of exploding on itself: it is
subversive."[34] He even considers the Liddell Hart history a "Borgesian"
work and cites passages from it which bear out his point that it is a more
fantastic account of the war "than any fiction an author could invent." Thus
he sums up the function of the frame—the "tainted" reality of Hart's questionable account—as serving "to lull the reader into a type of false security
as regards the status of 'real' events, a security he will be forced to give up
. . . in befuddlement."[35] This operation on the reader is accomplished by
"two parallel yet incompatible plots," that is, the detective story and the
metaphysical plot. In the detective plot, he explains, "the murder is a coded
message, the solution of which hinges on a semantic notion, that of elimination, and a key word, the name to express location." The other plot is also a
kind of detective story," though of a literary-critical nature," where again the
message is "Tsui Pen's will . . . which is decoded on the basis of the key
word *time,* which Tsui Pen *eliminated* from his novel." Thus the secondary
plot "parallels the murder plot in abstract form; both involve messages to be
decoded on the basis of the elimination of a key term."[36]

Rudy then pauses to examine Borges's well-known ideas on prose fiction
as expressed in his key essay of 1932, "El arte narrativo y la magia." He in-
terprets the basic idea contained in this text: "the emphasis on plot entails a
reduction in the importance of character and necessitates a concomitant increase in embedded, structurally significant details . . . which prefigure the
action and form a 'secret plot.' "[37] He then goes on to point out several of
these significant embedded details which in "El jardín" unify the two parallel plots: on the level of imagery, the use of circles, and on the level of plot,
Yu Tsun's meditation, early in the text, on his ancestor's labyrinth, or the

brief mention of his ancestor having been murdered by a stranger, a clear foreshadowing of the detective plot's climax.

Shlomith Rimmon-Kenan's well-written "Doubles and Counterparts: The Garden of the Forking Paths," first published in 1980 and reprinted in 1986 in Harold Bloom's volume on Borges in the "Modern Critical Views" series, is another excellent example of how recent critical approaches can shed light on canonical texts. Her opening paragraph is probably the most concise summation one can find of the story's structure: "That the governing structural principle of the 'Garden of the Forking Paths' is the analogy among fictional levels goes almost without saying. In the fashion of Chinese boxes many parallels are established between the characters of Yu Tsun, Stephen Albert and Tsui Pen."[38] But one of her richest discussions, later in her study, involves the way Borges achieves the disintegration of the concept of self or identity in this text. To illustrate this process she focuses upon analogy among characters and what she terms "the repetition of the act of narration." Her discussion of this point relies heavily on Genette's and other contemporary narratalogists' sophisticated diagetic categories. Thus she stresses "quotation" as the dominant narrative mode of the story. She notes that quotation is "the appropriation by one person of the speech of another," which in turn implies an "interpenetration of personalities," a clear threat to "the absolute autonomy of the self."[39] This is a provocative and debatable point, as even Rimmon-Kenan herself admits. She then concludes her piece by taking an opposite view and presenting some charmingly paradoxical ruminations, making her study "open-ended" in the best sense of the term.

The critical trajectory that Borges studies will follow in the future is not eassy to predict. On first glance, it appears that virtually everything that could be said has indeed been said. The biographical approach seems to have been exhausted by recent work; the detractors of Borges have had their day in court; bibliographers and indexers have painstakingly produced their useful volumes; and the new critics have brough fresh insights to bear on well-read texts. Yet Borges has left us a rich, complex, and, in many instances, an ambiguous body of writing. That recent scholarship can profitably reexamine his texts of the forties indicates that, as in the case of all great writers, the last word may never be said.

There is, moreover, a nice Borgesian irony in the fact that scholars and critics will in all probability continue to work on his texts. For Borges, despite the fact that he appreciated bibliophiles, cataloguers, and literary historians, and that he wrote some memorable critical pages himself, really had mixed feelings about academics and professional critics. While he relished the work of creative writers, he showed much less enthusiasm for those who sought fame or mere recognition by basking in the reflected glory of literary luminaries. In short, those who have worked on Borges should not forget that wonderful narrator of "Pierre Menard," that petulant, self-important, snide unnamed critic whose total identity was derived from a parasitic relationship to the Great Writer.

Chapter Five
Borges in Perspective

Almost twenty years ago a British commentator concluded his overview of Borges with the observation that the Argentine writer was a "consummate master of his own restricted territory and on that account a writer only a little less than great."[1] How valid was this assessment then and how valid is it now? The last decades of Borges's life witnessed the production of a number of fairly important stories and poems, but did the "new Borges" really add luster to the writer of the forties and fifties? I have already noted the role he played in shaping some of the dominant critical thought of our times: yet his impact in this area has become fully apparent only in the last two decades. And what can be said about his influence on other writers present and future? In short, how meaningful will the adjective "Borgesian" be as the years pass?

Critics, myself included, have on occasion spoken of the "old" versus the "new" Borges. As noted early in chapter 3, periods in an author's career have an organizational value but, more often than not, they do not have any greater reality. This is amply confirmed in Borges's case. His fundamental literary tenets, his interest in certain philosophical notions, and the affective range found in his works really changed little over the years. Thus what may appear to have been one of the few shifts in his approach to fiction—the seemingly simpler, less erudite, and more allegorical emphasis of certain stories in *Doctor Brodie's Report*—in retrospect seems only superficial and, in addition, quite short-lived. Although the best of this group of tales—"The Gospel according to St. Mark," "Guayaquil," and conceivably "The Intruder"—may stand on their own merits, one wonders what their fate would have been had they been submitted for publication by an unknown author. Another rich text of the later period, "The Congress," underscores a similar problem. If one is familiar with Borges's work, it is an amusing, playful piece full of irony and intratextual winks at the reader. However, a reader approaching "The Congress" as a first taste of Borges's fiction would probably find it confusing, ill-conceived, or perhaps boring. The point is that much of Borges's work is interdependent: our appreciation, understanding, and aesthetic pleasure upon reading one text is enhanced by our experience with other texts. His admitted self-plagiarism (condemned by critics in the forties and now legitimized as intratextuality), his constant reworking of the same themes, and a host of frequently repeated minor stylistic details allow us to recognize a "Borgesian" passage with little difficulty, in somewhat the same way that a music lover can usually identify a phrase of Bach or Mozart. This situation tends to make his readers—and critics— more appreciative of his total corpus of work and more tolerant of the weaker pieces, a good many of which are found in his later books.

With regard to Borges's overall achievement, it remains clear that his most significant work was done in the forties and fifties and that it consists of the canonical short narratives, many of which I discuss in chapter 2. It is also safe to say that despite the undeniable quality of his poetry—even much of the later work—he made his mark as a writer of prose. His verse, to put matters in the same logical terms that Borges applied to literary history, will be "contingent" while his prose is "necessary." That is, no present-day writer of Spanish fiction can put pen to paper without echoing Borges, without attempting to transcend Borges, or at the least, without thinking of Borges.

His essays, especially those dealing with literary questions, might be almost as important, almost as "necessary," as the canonical fiction. Though written in a deceptively casual style, many of these are laden with ideas that have exercised, as we have seen, a surprisingly strong influence on contemporary critical thought: I refer to such pieces as "Kafka and His Precursors," "Partial Magic in the Quixote," "A Note on (toward) Bernard Shaw," "The Fearful Sphere of Pascal," "The Analytical Language of John Wilkins," and the notes on Valéry, Hawthorne, and Coleridge. Their impact, in my view, has been especially great in that they are often reinforced by Borges's own literary practice. The use of second- (or even third-) level narrators discussed in "Partial Magic in the Quixote," to mention only one example, is a common feature in Borges's own fiction; many other illustrations could easily be found.

A measure of any major writer's significance is the degree to which he influences others. I have already alluded to this above noting that anyone writing Spanish prose must, in some way, take Borges into account. His presence is especially strong in the case of Spanish America's "new narrative"—the celebrated blossoming of the continent's prose fiction in the late fifties and sixties. Anyone who has carefully read Julio Cortázar, Nobel laureate Gabriel García Márquez, Carlos Fuentes, and the others cannot help but sense, on occasion, certain affinities and echoes of a "Borgesian" nature in these authors. But leaving aside textual considerations, in a broader sense Borges has played an important role in making the new narrative and the associated "boom" of Spanish American literature possible. He did this simply by gaining an unprecedented degree of recognition, not for the documentary or picturesque nature of his writing, but for the sheer aesthetic quality of his work. In this respect, especially when the international diffusion of his work is taken into account, Borges was a pioneer: no Spanish American writer before him had achieved anything like the position he enjoyed as early as the sixties. Strong support for this point is given by Chile's leading novelist, José Donoso. In his very informative account of the new narrative's blossoming, *Historia personal del boom* (1972), he discusses the significance of the worldwide acclaim accorded Borges: "the appearance of this mature, continental, international public . . . changed radically the environment toward the mid sixties; now the audience for novelists was not limited to their own country, but included the entire Spanish-speaking world. This public was interested, it was now clear, in literature as such, and not as an extension of pedagogy, patriotism, or reporting. This became evident with the sudden popularity of Borges following his 'discovery' in the United States, Italy and France."[2] Thus, with the "phenomenon" of Borges, readers on both sides of the Atlantic were forced to revise what one critic has called "the conventional image of Spanish America."[3] In short, after him it was easier to read Latin American literature free of inhibiting stereotypes.[4]

That Borges has been a major point of reference for the writers of the new narrative can be easily documented. Jaime Alazraki, in an essay entitled "Borges and the New Latin American Novel," shows that even those writers who attacked him, such as the Argentine novelist Ernesto Sábato, accept him as a mentor and even adopt some of his techniques.[5] The same observer notes that Borges's treatment of the fantastic, which is an important element in the new narrative, differs basically from the way it had traditionally been handled since the days of the *modernistas*. It was the Borgesian technique of creating a bridge between the real and the unreal, of "effacing the borderline between the two"[6] that was adopted by a number of these writers. This is seen clearly in Julio Cortázar, who has often admitted his debt to Borges, despite the fact that his overall concept of literature differs greatly from that of his compatriot. Alazraki's comments are well taken: if one compares, for example, the basic structure of Borges's celebrated tale "The South" (1953) with any number of Cortázar's almost formulaic stories involving parallel planes of time and space, the similarity between the two writers becomes obvious.

Critics have also noted the Borgesian mode in Gabriel García Márquez's masterpiece, *One Hundred Years of Solitude*. The strongest case for linking the two, in my view, is seen in the underlying narrative frame of the Colombian's novel: both the reader and one of the book's chief characters learn at the end that the story itself had been written earlier by one of its minor personages, the mysterious gypsy Melquíades. Thus, the novel is really a story within a story—one of Borges's favorite gambits—as is the confusion of author and character. Of course these literary games are not recent inventions. Borges himself was sufficiently fascinated by them to discuss these techniques in Cervantes and others, as in the previously noted essay "Partial Magic in the Quixote." There are a number of other specific points of contact between the work of the two writers, but perhaps the most important Borgesian influence that can be found in Spanish American letters lies in the areas of style and language. As Alazraki observes, "I believe contemporary Spanish American fiction, consciously or unconsciously, willingly or unwillingly, is marked by a prose that did not exist before Borges." García Márquez himself speaks of his "extraordinary capacity for verbal artifice," of how reading Borges "tune[s] up your instrument for saying things."[7] A chance remark by an Argentine novelist of some repute, Alberto Vanasco, gives informal but eloquent testimony to his compatriot's influence on literary language: in a conversation with a North American academic, Gene Bell-Villada, he stated simply, "Before Borges one could write sloppily. But not anymore."[8]

Borges himself often described what he considered to be the exemplar of good style. An early (1928) statement on the subject is very clear: "Total effectiveness and total invisibility should be the twin aims of style."[9] It should be emphasized, moreover, that despite the complexity of some of his plots, despite the sophistication of his narrative strategies, and despite his penchant for literary or philosophical esoterica, on the strictly stylistic level he usually practiced what he preached. In short, his style is almost always clear, precise, often diaphanous. His views in this regard have been likened to those of Albert Camus or to Roland Barthes's exhortation to authors to abandon the verbosity and ornament of yesteryear for direct, bare-bones "neutral writing." Thus Alazraki believes "if it is true that the tradition of highly wrought language came to Latin America primarily from France, it is no less true that through Borges Spanish American novelists rid themselves of estheticism much earlier than the French, who only did so, led by Camus, in the late forties."[10]

In addition to his influence upon Latin American writers and his relationship to contemporary literary theorists, Borges's presence has also been noted in the work of several North American writers, in Vladimir

Nabokov, and in certain French novelists.[11] If one were to list all the cases of specific influences along with those of close aesthetic kinship, how might this group of writers be described? In the attempt to define the form and spirit of contemporary letters, especially its radical "different-ness" from traditional writing, recent commentators have seized upon the term *postmodern*. Among the many authors deemed postmodernists (Samuel Beckett, Italo Calvino, Alain Robbe-Grillet, Thomas Pynchon, John Barth, Julio Cortázar, etc.), the name of Jorge Luis Borges often appears. In fact, Douwe Fokkema, a leading European student of this movement—or "literary code," as he calls it—has stated that "the writer who has contributed more than anyone else to the invention and accept-ance of the new code is Jorge Luis Borges."[12] Admittedly the term itself is very broad, ill-defined, and self-destructive in that one of the frequently stated characteristics of the postmodern attitude is its rejection of any defi-nition, of being neatly pigeonholed.[13] Placed in the context of post-modernism, Borges occupies an ambiguous position, for again, a great deal depends upon what defining characteristics one accepts for the move-ment. Clearly his work does not partake of the pop art aspect or of the kitsch associated with some postmodernist art. In fact, his style, his lexi-con, and many of his attitudes seem very old-fashioned—more pre-modernist than postmodernist. Yet there are many well-defined features of his writing that appear to be paradigmatic expressions of postmodern-ism. For example, a hallmark of his fiction (and of his poetry for that mat-ter) is its circularity, its reliance upon repetition, a feature frequently associated with postmodernism. As one European critic observes, "There is no progress, only repetition. Accordingly narration is not teleological but circular." He then cites as examples Nabokov, Robbe-Grillet, and Barth: Borges, he notes, was an earlier precursor of this kind of fiction.[14] Another very Borgesian structural feature, that of the bifurcating or mul-tiple plot, has also been linked with the postmodern aesthetic. In her dis-cussion of these "multiple narrative instances," one student of contemporary letters states that while it is common in the work of Nabokov, Barth, and others, it is "an idea originally lined out by Borges."[15] On a more general level, the critic Ihab Hassan notes, a basic characteristic of postmodernism is "fragmentation"—literature as bits and pieces rather than as an integrated totality.[16] In a sense the entire corpus of Borges's work is just that; after all, here is a master narrator who has never written a novel, who has serious reservations about this genre, and whose individual fictional compositions range from a few paragraphs in length to no more than fifteen or twenty pages. Of course, there is a Borgesian irony

in that these fragments strike us as being part of a hidden matrix: thus his
"bits and pieces" invite the reader to search for a synthesis. Another point
made by Hassan concerns "hybridization," defined as "the mutant replica-
tion of genres, including parody . . . the deformation of genres [that] en-
genders equivocal modes." In this context he refers specifically to Borges's
Pierre Menard as exemplifying how "an image or replica may be as valid as
its model."[17] The same critic considers reflexiveness and "an ironic access
or excess of self-consciousness" as other common postmodern features:
again, these terms clearly suggest Borges's writing.

   This notion of ironic self-consciousness leads to the broader issue of
metafiction, of a fiction whose central concern is the creation of fiction itself.
Whether or not metafiction is a characteristic of postmodernism may be
moot (I think it is, despite its roots in the seventeenth and eighteenth centuries); however, there is no question that a number of critics have singled
out Borges as a major practitioner of this literary mode. Chief among these
commentators is Robert Alter, who in his widely read *Partial Magic: The
Novel as a Self-Conscious Genre* (1975) discusses Borges in some detail. The
very title of Alter's book comes from Borges's essay "Partial Magic in the
Quixote." Although his study is not centered on the Argentine writer or on
postmodernism, a term he uses only sparingly toward the end of his book,
in his final chapter Alter does offer some trenchant remarks regarding both.
Speaking of literature at the mid-century mark, he finds that the "high tide"
of modernism has passed and that some of the writers of the new self-
conscious fiction have followed Borges in producing "fictions" rather than
traditional short stories. He then discusses, in very critical terms, the nascent
postmodernism of the times, noting its strengths and especially its weak-
nesses: self-indulgence, pointless gamesmanship, and the loss of the vital
tension between reality and literary artifice. He knowingly points out that
some of the most dubious work of the postmodernists has been promoted
by brilliant critics—such as George Steiner and Roland Barthes—whose
commentary is often more impressive than the texts they analyze. Alter
senses that literature, especially the novel, may be in a real state of crisis; to
help clarify the situation he turns to the novelist John Barth, and specifically
to his celebrated essay of 1967, "The Literature of Exhaustion," centered on
Beckett, Nabokov, and Borges. While Alter seems to agree with Barth's
choice of the Argentine as the best example of the "used-upness" of literary
possibilities, he takes issue with the essay's implication that, in effect, there
is nothing left to write (Alter even shows how Barth tries to extricate himself
from this untenable position). For our purposes, however, Alter's most telling remarks are directed at the specific choice of Borges as the "paradig-

matic postmodernist." His position is well taken and offers a balanced view of Borges's relationship to contemporary letters, and in particular to the novel:

The choice of Borges as the paradigmatic postmodernist is in one respect misleading precisely because Borges the prose-writer is an inventor of parables and paradoxes, not a novelist. That is, Borges of the *ficciones* is concerned with a series of metaphysical enigmas about identity, recurrence, cyclicality, time, thought, and extension, and so it is a little dangerous to translate his haunting fables into allegories of the postmodern literary situation. . . . The fact that Borges is a fabulist, not a novelist, hardly suggests that the fable is all there remains for fiction to work with now. Were he a novelist, his prototypical protagonist would not be a meditative wraith wandering through the hexagonal mazes of the infinite Library of Babel, but a man or woman—one glimpses the possibility in his most recent stories—with a distinctive psychology living among other men and women, acting against a background of social values, personal and national history. Such a figure, it seems safe to assume, would have a rather different relationship to the written word, past and present, than does the inhabitant of the great Library or the assiduous Pierre Menard.[18]

Before leaving the Alter-Barth exchange and the issue of Borges as a postmodernist, I must mention Barth's more recent views. In an essay of 1980, "The Literature of Replenishment," the American novelist suggests that his earlier article was "much misread" (even by Borges himself) and that he never wished to suggest that fiction had in fact reached a dead end. Rather, "artistic conventions are liable to be retired, subverted, transcended, or even deployed against themselves to generate new and lively work."[19] His point in the essay is simply that literature by the mid-century seemed to have reached a turning point where "high modernism" (read Pound, Joyce, et al.) had completed its program and where a new direction was in order. It was at this juncture that Borges is to be found: "As Cervantes stands as an exemplar of premodernism and a great precursor of much to come . . . Jorge Luis Borges [stands] as an exemplar of *dernier cri* modernism and at the same time as a bridge between the end of the nineteenth century and the end of the twentieth."[20]

That Borges has had a major impact on contemporary letters as well as on recent trends in literary theory seems amply demonstrated. But aside from considerations of influence, the question of his intrinsic value as a writer has not been fully answered. This chapter began with the comment that Borges might be "only a little less than great." Robert Alter, while acknowledging his catalytic influence on contemporary writers of fiction, reveals some reservations about this bookish "fabulist" and writer of fictions who never came to grips with the novel, the genre almost synonymous with modern literature itself. Finally, Borges never won the Nobel Prize; although the explanation of this may be political, the fact remains that he was denied the award.[21] Mildly conservative (or "liberal" in the nineteenth-century sense), Borges abjured "commitment" in his writing. In addition, many have considered him lacking in humanity and as escaping reality for a world of books. There may be some truth in these charges, but I would suggest that those who hold these views read some of his best poetry or some of the very intimate parables in collections like *Dreamtigers*. And if laughter is any indication of humanity, I would invite the doubters to reread any number of the great ironic texts of his canonical period. Lastly, I think that Borges, now beyond the final Hexagon of the Library, would smile with amusement at our efforts to justify or vindicate (to use another favorite term) his greatness. For the writer who denied literary originality and who questioned the pretentions of authorship, the entire issue is not all that important. After all, literature is only a game of put and take and to have been one of the players—and a rather good one at that—may be reward enough.

Notes and References

Chapter One

1. Jorge Luis Borges, *Atlas,* trans. and annot. Anthony Kerrigan (New York: Dutton, 1985), 38.
2. Ibid., 54.
3. Alicia Jurado, *Genio y figura de Jorge Luis Borges* (Buenos Aires: Edit. Universitaria de Buenos Aires, 1964), 51.
4. Cited by Gloria Videla, *El ultraísmo* (Madrid: Gredos, 1963), 201.
5. Jorge Luis Borges, *Obra poética* (Buenos Aires: Emecé, 1964), 39. Although later editions of the *Obra poética* have been published, I have chosen the 1964 edition for citation of the earlier poetry because the texts are much closer to those of the original collections. Borges and/or his editors have constantly made minor changes, omissions, etc. in the various editions of his poetry; when important, these will be noted. Succeeding references to the early poetry are noted parenthetically in the text as OP 64. Unless otherwise noted, the translations are my own.
6. Videla, *Ultraísmo,* 201.
7. "Ultraísmo," *Nosotros* 151 (December 1921): 466–71.
8. Jorge Luis Borges, *Macedonio Fernández* (Buenos Aires: Edit. Culturales Argentinas, 1961), 20.
9. Ibid.
10. Borges, "Ultraísmo," 466–71.
11. This poem does not appear in later editions of the *Obra poética.*
12. An interesting example of the poetry suppressed in later editions is "Llamarada." The piece is actually a prose poem, quite confessional, and even a bit erotic. Note the line, "deseando . . . perdernos en las culminaciones carnales."
13. Jorge Luis Borges, *Luna de enfrente* (Buenos Aires: Proa, 1925), 7.
14. Jorge Luis Borges, *Poemas: 1923–1958* (Buenos Aires: Emecé, 1958), 82. Although it appears in the original and in this 1958 collection, "Monterideo" is omitted from later editions of the *Obra poética.*
15. Jorge Luis Borges, "Contestación a la encuesta sobre la nueva generación literaria," *Nosotros* 168 (May 1923): 16–17.
16. For further information on Fernández, see Borges's own *Macedonio Fernández* (note 8).
17. Jorge Luis Borges, *Inquisiciones* (Buenos Aires: Proa, 1925), 91.
18. Ibid., 114–15.
19. Jorge Luis Borges, *El tamaño de mi esperanza* (Buenos Aires: Proa, 1926), 100.

20. Jorge Luis Borges, *El idioma de los argentinos* (Buenos Aires: M. Gleizer, 1928), 102.

21. Ibid., 147–48.

22. Jorges Luis Borges, *Discusión* (Buenos Aires: M. Gleizer, 1930), 58. Succeeding references to this work are noted parenthetically in the text as *D*.

23. Jorge Luis Borges, *Other Inquisitions 1937–52,* trans. Ruth L. C. Simms with an introduction by J. E. Irby (Austin: University of Texas Press, 1964), 171. Succeeding references are noted parenthetically in the text as *OI*.

24. Jorge Luis Borges, "Libros y autores extranjeros. Guía de lectores," *Revista Hogar,* 22 January 1937, 30. Borges's book reviews in this publication have recently been collected in a single volume edited by Enrique Sacerio–Garí and Emir Rodríguez Monegal, *Textos cautivos* (Buenos Aires: Tusquets, 1986).

25. Jorge Luis Borges, "La última invención de Hugh Walpole," *La Nación,* 10 January 1943, 30.

Chapter Two

1. Jorge Luis Borges, *A Universal History of Infamy,* trans. Norman Thomas di Giovanni (New York: Dutton, 1972), 13. Succeeding references are noted parenthetically in the text as *UHI*.

2. Emir Rodríguez Monegal, *Jorge Luis Borges: A Literary Biography* (New York: Dutton, 1978), 244.

3. Note, as indicative of his mood, the "Two English Poems" discussed in the previous chapter.

4. Regarding these items, see chapter 1, note 24.

5. There are a number of versions of the accident. Cf. Rodríguez Monegal, *Borges: A Literary Biography,* 320–22; Jurado, *Genio y figura,* 42; and Borges's own "An Autobiographical Essay" appended to *The Aleph and Other Stories,* trans. Norman Thomas di Giovanni (New York: Dutton, 1978), 242–43.

6. Cited by Ronald Christ in "The Art of Fiction: Jorge Luis Borges," *Paris Review* 40 (1967):124.

7. Jorge Luis Borges, *A Personal Anthology,* ed. with a foreword by Anthony Kerrigan (New York: Grove, 1967), 23. Succeeding references are noted parenthetically in the text as *PA*.

8. Jorge Luis Borges, *Labyrinths: Selected Stories and Other Writings,* ed. Donald A. Yates and James E. Irby (New York: New Directions, 1962), 45. Although other translations of these texts are, in some cases, available, I have chosen to use those appearing in *Labyrinths* because they have had very wide circulation and, for English readers, have become "canonical" translations. Succeeding references to works appearing in this collection are noted parenthetically in the text as *L*.

9. On this technique, see the perceptive discussion in Silvia Molloy's *Las letras de Borges* (Buenos Aires: Sudamericana, 1979), 234.

10. For an analysis of these texts, see my *Jorge Luis Borges* (New York: Twayne, 1970), 118–19 and 129–32.

11. Borges's penchant for creating an interlocking system of apocryphal names is well illustrated here. Another text of this collection, "Three Versions of Judas," centers about the life and works of a fictitious scholar named Nils Runeberg. With two Runebergs in the same collection, the reader begins to assume their reality. Note also the meaning of "rune," and old Scandinavian word denoting "a secret, a mystery," and by extension, a letter of the alphabet or a cipher.

12. For an interesting discussion of this and related techniques, see Molloy, *Letras,* 119–20, 166, 175–76.

13. On this point, see Roslyn M. Frank and Nancy Vosburg, "Textos y Contra-Textos en 'El jardín de senderos que se bifurcan,' " *Revista Iberoamericana* 100–101 (1977): 326.

14. Shilomith Rimmon-Kenan, "Doubles and Counterparts: 'The Garden of the Forking Paths,' " in *Modern Critical Views: Jorge Luis Borges,* ed. with an introduction by Harold Bloom (New York: Chelsea House, 1986), 191.

15. Jorge Luis Borges, *The Aleph and Other Stories 1933–1969,* ed. and trans. Norman Thomas di Giovanni (New York: Dutton, 1970), 81. Succeeding references are noted parenthetically in the text as *AOS.*

16. A curious slip here—perhaps intentional—in that Borges uses the dieresis over the *o*. This would naturally increase the total number of possibilities in the Library, as Borges specifically states that only the comma, period, space, and the regular alphabet constitute its orthographic elements. See *Labyrinths,* 53n.

17. James E. Irby, "Borges and the Idea of Utopia," in Bloom, *Critical Views: Borges,* 93–94. This essay also appears in *The Cardinal Points of Borges* edited by Lowell Dunham and Ivan Ivask (Norman: University of Oklahoma Press, 1970).

18. The three writers were, of course, very real, well-known figures. Alfonso Reyes was a highly regarded Mexican essayist and humanist, Ezéquiel Martínez Estrada, an Argentine poet and essayist, and Nestor Ibarra, a Franco-Argentine critic.

19. Though hardly an activist, Borges did take strong political positions. Regarding some of these, see Rodríguez Mongeal, *Borges: A Literary Biography,* 296–305, 344–46, 391–93. For a general view of the political situation of Argentine writers during these years, see my "Argentine Letters and the Peronato: An Overview," *Journal of Inter-American Studies and World Affairs* 3–4 (1971): 434–55.

20. John Dominic Crossan, *Raid on the Articulate: Comic Eschatology in Jesus and Borges* (New York: Harper & Row, 1976). This work's title is from the book's epigraph: "And so each venture is a new beginning, a raid on the articulate" (from T. S. Eliot's *East Coker*).

21. Many critics have noted Borges's penchant for the color red and have commented on its obvious—and at times less obvious—symbolism. A particularly rich discussion of this point appears in Carter Wheelock's *The Mythmaker: A Study of Motif and Symbol in the Short Stories of Jorge Luis Borges* (Austin: University of Texas Press, 1969).

22. Jorge Luis Borges, *El Aleph* (Buenos Aires: Losada, 1949), 140–41. In this case, I use my own translation because the di Giovanni version (see note 15) departs substantially from the original Spanish of this passage.

23. The point is confirmed by María Esther Vázquez, a close friend and collaborator of Borges. In an interview with him she reports Borges as saying that he wrote the story "riéndome porque me causaba mucha gracia." See her "Entrevista" appended to Borges's *Veinticinco agosto 1983 y otros cuentos* (Madrid: Siruela, 1983), 72.

Chapter Three

1. See note 19, chapter 2.

2. Regarding his first marriage and other biographical details through the late seventies, see Rodríguez Monegal, *Borges: A Literary Biography,* 470–76.

3. Other volumes that have served a similar purpose are his *Antología personal* (1961) and the *Nueva antología personal* (1969).

4. Miguel Enguídanos, "Introduction to Jorge Luis Borges," *Dreamtigers*, trans. Mildred Boyer and Harold Morland (Austin: University of Texas Press, 1964), 14. Succeeding references appear parenthetically in the text as *Dt.*

5. Cited by Ana María Barrenechea in *La expresión de la irrealidad en la obra de Jorge Luis Borges* (Mexico: Colegio de México, 1957), 10. The translation is from Robert Lima's *Borges the Labyrinth Maker* (New York: New York University Press, 1965), 17.

6. Borges's publisher, Editorial Emecé, however, published a later separate volume of poetry titled *El otro, el mismo* (Buenos Aires: Emecé, 1969).

7. Jorge Luis Borges, *Obra poética: 1923–76* (Madrid and Buenos Aires: Alianza-Emecé, 1979), 194–95. Succeeding references appear parenthetically in the text as *OP.* Some of the later poetry has been translated in *Selected Poems 1923–67,* ed. with an introduction by Norman Thomas di Giovanni (New York: Delacorte Press, 1972). The translations in my text are, however, my own, though they occasionally parallel the published versions quite closely.

8. Jorge Luis Borges, *In Praise of Darkness,* trans. Norman Thomas di Giovanni (New York: Dutton, 1974), 10. Succeeding references appear parenthetically in the text as *PD.* In this case I have retained di Giovanni's translations.

9. Jorge Luis Borges, *The Gold of the Tigers: Selected Later Poems; Bilingual Edition,* trans. Alastair Reid (New York: Dutton, 1977), 7. Succeeding references appear parenthetically as *GT.* I have retained Reid's translations in my text.

10. Jorge Luis Borges, *Historia de la noche* (Buenos Aires: Emecé, 1977), 91.

11. Ricardo Jaimes Freyre (1868–1933) of Bolivia was an important poet of the *modernista* movement; Luis de León (1527–1591) was a major poet and theologian of Spain's Golden Age.

12. Jorge Luis Borges, *La cifra* (Madrid: Alianza, 1981), 12. Succeeding references appear parenthetically in the text as *C.*

13. Jorge Luis Borges, *Los conjurados* (Madrid: Alianza, 1985), 63. Succeeding references appear parenthetically in the text as *Co.*

14. Jorge Luis Borges, *Doctor Brodie's Report,* trans. Norman Thomas di Giovanni in collaboration with the author (New York: Bantam Books, 1972), 9. Succeeding references appear parenthetically in the text as *BR.*

15. Rodríguez Monegal, *Borges: A Literary Biography,* 464.

16. Carter Wheelock, "Borges's New Prose" in Bloom, *Critical Views: Borges,* 113.

17. Ibid., 122.

18. Gene H. Bell-Villada, *Borges and His Fiction: A Guide to His Mind and Art* (Chapel Hill: University of North Carolina Press, 1981), 254.

19. Rodríguez Monegal, *Borges: A Literary Biography,* 464.

20. Bell-Villada, *Borges,* 255–56.

21. Jorge Luis Borges, *The Book of Sand,* trans. Norman Thomas di Grovanni (New York: Dutton, 1977), 34. Succeeding references appear parenthetically in the text as *BS.*

22. Cf. my interpretation with those of Wheelock, "Borges's New Prose," 126–30, and Rodríguez Monegal, *Borges: A Literary Biography,* 464.

23. Rodríguez Monegal, *Borges: A Literary Biography,* 464.

24. Jorge Luis Borges, *Veinticinco agosto 1983 y otros cuentos* (Madrid: Siruela, 1983), 13.

25. Ibid., 16.

26. Again I must point out that Borges's collaborative work—an important facet of his total production—is not discussed in this study. However, for a listing of these works, see the *Selected Bibliography.*

27. Jorge Luis Borges, *Atlas,* 48.

Chapter Four

1. Ernesto Sábato, "Desagravio a Borges," *Sur* 94 (July 1942): 7–34.

2. Adolfo Prieto, *Borges y la nueva generación* (Buenos Aires: Letras Universitarias, 1954), 18.

3. Ibid., 70–1.

4. Ana María Barrenechea, *Borges the Labyrinth Maker,* trans. Robert Lima (New York: New York University Press, 1965), 16.

5. Ibid., 144.

6. For an excellent discussion of Borges's early reception in France, see Silvia Molloy, *La diffusion de la littérature hispano-américaine en France au XX siècle* (Paris: Presses Universitaires de France, 1972), 194–247.

7. Paul de Man, "A Modern Master" in Bloom, *Critical Views: Borges,* 21–27. The original appeared in the *New York Review of Books* 5 November 1964.

8. John Updike, "Books: The Author as Librarian," *New Yorker,* 30 October 1965, 223.

9. Ibid.

10. Ibid., 246.

11. John Barth, "The Literature of Exhaustion," *Atlantic,* August 1967, 30.

12. Ibid.

13. Ibid., 33.

14. Molloy, *Diffusion,* 205–206.

15. John D. Crossan, *Raid,* 77.

16. Ernesto Sábato, "En torno a Borges," *Casa de las Américas* 17–18 (1963): 7–12.

17. Camilo José Cela, "Buenos Aires o un mar sin orillas," *Indice* 59 (1953):2

18. Noé Jitrik, "Estructura y significación en *Ficciones* de Jorge Luis Borges," *Casa de las Américas* 53 (1969):56. This article is reprinted in Jitrik's *El fuego de la especie* and in Juan Fló's *Contra Borges.*

19. Ibid., 62.

20. Peter Caws, "Structuralism" in *Dictionary of the History of Ideas,* ed. P. P. Wiener (New York: Scribners, 1973), vol.4:326. See also David W. Foster, "Borges and Structuralism: Toward an Implied Poetics," *Modern Fiction Studies* 19 (1973):345.

21. Cited by Emir Rodríguez Monegal in "Borges y nouvelle critique," *Revista Iberoamericana* 80 (1972):367 (epigraph).

22. Foster, "Borges and Structuralism," 343.

23. Rodríguez Monegal, "Borges. y nouvelle critique," 369.

24. Gérard Genette, *Figures* (Paris: Ed. du Seuil, 1966), 164.

25. Ibid., 169.

26. Michel Foucault, "Preface" to *The Order of Things* (New York: Vintage, 1973), xv.

27. See chapter 1.

28. Foucault, "Preface," xvii.

29. Michel Foucault, *Language, Counter-Memory, Practice* (Ithaca, N.Y.: Cornell University Press, 1977), 54.

30. See David W. Foster's *Studies in the Contemporary Spanish-American Short Story* (Columbia: University of Missouri Press, 1979), 18, n.12.

31. Roberto González Echeverria, "Borges and Derrida," in Bloom, *Critical Views: Borges,* 227–34.

32. John Sturrock, *Paper Tigers: The Ideal Fictions of Jorge Luis Borges* (Oxford: Clarendon, 1977), 203.

33. Stephen Rudy, "The Garden *of* and *in* Borges's 'Garden of the Forking Paths' " in *The Structural Analysis of Narrative Texts,* ed. A. Kodjak and others (Columbus, O.: Slavica, 1980), 132.

34. Ibid., 133.

35. Ibid., 135.

36. Ibid., 137.

37. Ibid., 139.

38. Shlomith Rimmon-Kenan, "Doubles and Counterparts: The Garden of the Forking Paths," in Bloom, *Critical Views: Borges*, 185.
39. Ibid., 191.

Chapter Five

1. J. M. Cohen, *Borges* (New York: Barnes and Noble, 1974), 111.
2. José Donoso, *The Boom in Spanish American Literature: A Personal History*, trans. G. Kolovakas (New York: Columbia University Press, 1977), 66–67.
3. Molloy, *Diffusion*, 107.
4. This point is developed at some length by González Echeverría in his "Borges and Derrida" in Bloom, *Critical Views: Borges*, 231–32.
5. Jaime Alazraki, "Borges and the New Latin American Novel," *TriQuarterly* 25 (1972): 382.
6. Ibid., 384.
7. Ibid., 390–1.
8. Cited by Bell-Villada, *Borges*, 275.
9. Alazraki, "Borges and the Novel," 393.
10. Ibid., 394.
11. For his impact on French writers, see Molloy, *Diffusion*, 194–237; for his influence on American fiction, see Ronald J. Christ, "Forking Narratives" in *Simply a Man of Letters* (Orono: University of Maine Press, 1982).
12. Douwe W. Fokkema, *Literary History, Modernism and Postmodernism* (Amsterdam and Philadelphia: J. Benjamins, 1984), 38. It is of some interest that Fokkema, in speaking of Borges, notes that postmodernism was the first "literary code" to have begun in the Western Hemisphere and subsequently influenced European letters.
13. Ihab Hassan, "Pluralism in Modern Perspective" in *Exploring Postmodernism*, ed. Douwe W. Fokkema (Amsterdam and Philadelphia, J. Benjamins, 1987), 18.
14. Mihály Szegedy-Maszák, "Teleology in Postmodern Fiction" in *Exploring Postmodernism*, 47.
15. Ulla Musarra, "Narrative Discourse in Postmodernist Texts," in *Exploring Postmodernism*, 224.
16. Hassan, "Pluralism," 19.
17. Ibid., 21.
18. Robert Alter, *Partial Magic: The Novel as a Self-Conscious Genre* (Berkeley, Los Angeles, and London: University of California Press, 1975), 227–28.
19. John Barth, "The Literature of Replenishment," *Atlantic*, January 1980, 71.
20. Ibid.
21. For further discussion of the Nobel prize issue, see Bell-Villada, *Borges*, chapter 11.

Selected Bibliography

PRIMARY WORKS

The listing below includes all major original editions and some of the most important collections of Borges's work. No definitive *Obras completas* (Complete Works) exists, though this title has been used by the Emecé publishing house for a series of several volumes as well as for a single-volume work of 1974. The Bruguera house of Barcelona published a two-volume *Prosa completa* in 1980 and an augmented edition of four volumes in 1985, but here again some material is lacking. For details on second editions, re-editions, and collected works, see D. W. Foster's *Jorge Luis Borges: An Annotated Primary and Secondary Bibliography*, listed below under Secondary Sources.

Narrative Prose

El Aleph. Buenos Aires: Losada, 1949.
Ficciones (1935–1944). Buenos Aires: Sur, 1944.
Historia universal de la infamia. Buenos Aires: Tor, 1935.
El informe de Brodie. Buenos Aires: Emecé, 1970.
El jardín de senderos que se bifurcan. Buenos Aires: Sur, 1941.
El libro de arena. Buenos Aires: Emecé, 1975.
Vienticinco agosto 1983 y otros cuentos. Madrid: Siruela, 1983.

Poetry

La cifra. Buenos Aires: Emecé, 1981.
Los conjurados. Madrid: Alianza, 1985.
Cuaderno San Martín. Buenos Aires: Proa, 1929.
Elogio de la sombra. Buenos Aires: Emecé, 1969.
Fervor de Buenos Aires. Buenos Aires: Imp. Serantes, 1923.
Historia de la noche. Buenos Aires: Emecé, 1977.
Luna de enfrente. Buenos Aires: Proa, 1925.
La moneda de hierro. Buenos Aires: Emecé, 1976.
Obra poética (1923–1964). Buenos Aires: Emecé, 1964. Augumented edition of vol. 2 of the Emecé *Obras completas*. Not an original work, but a convenient source for the texts of the now rare editions of the early poetry.

Obra poética: 1923–1976. Madrid: Alianza; Buenos Aires: Emecé, 1979. Not an original title but a convenient source for poetry of the period.
El otro, el mismo. Buenos Aires: Emecé, 1969.
Para las seis cuerdas. Buenos Aires: Emecé, 1965.
La rosa profunda. Buenos Aires: Emecé, 1975.

Essays

Discusión. Buenos Aires: M. Gleizer, 1932.
Evaristo Carriego. Buenos Aires: M. Gleizer, 1930. A literary biography of this Argentine poet, with considerable essayistic material.
Historia de la eternidad. Buenos Aires: Viau y Zona, 1936.
El idioma de los argentinos. Buenos Aires: M. Gleizer, 1928.
Inquisiciones. Buenos Aires: Proa, 1925.
Nueva refutación del tiempo. Buenos Aires: Oportet y Haereses, 1947. A single essay.
Nueve ensayos dantescos. Madrid: Espasa-Calpe, 1982.
Otras inquisiciones (1937–1952). Buenos Aires: Sur, 1952.
Prólogos, con un prólogo de prólogos. Buenos Aires: Torres Agüero, 1975. Not an original work, but a very valuable and convenient collection of prologues to books often difficult to obtain.
El tamaño de mi esperanza. Buenos Aires: Proa, 1926.
Textos cautivos: Ensayos y reseños en "El Hogar." Edited by E. Sacerio-Garí and E. Rodríguez Monegal. Buenos Aires: Tusquets, 1986. Not an original work, but a valuable collection of Borges's previously uncollected essays and reviews from the Argentine magazine *El Hogar.*

Prose and Poetry

Antología personal. Buenos Aires: Sur, 1961. The author's selection of his previously published pieces.
Los conjurados. Madrid: Alianza, 1985.
El hacedor. Buenos Aires: Emecé, 1960.
Libro de sueños. Buenos Aires: Torres Agüero, 1976. A predominantly prose anthology of short texts by other writers, glosses by Borges, and some original texts all describing dreams or comments on dreams.
Nueva antología personal. Buenos Aires: Emecé, 1968. Another author's selection of his previously published pieces.
El oro de los tigres. Buenos Aires: Emecé, 1972.

Narrative Prose in Collaboration

Dos fantasías memorables. H. Bustos Domecq (pseud. of J. L. Borges and A. Bioy Casares). Buenos Aires: Oportet and Haereses, 1946.

La hermana de Eloisa. With Luisa Mercedes Levinson. Buenos Aires: Ene, 1955. Individual stories by each author; title story in collaboration.
Um modelo para la muerte. B. Suárez Lynch (pseud. of J. L. Borges and A. Bioy Casares). Buenos Aires: Oportet and Haereses, 1946.
Nuevos cuentos de Bustos Domecq. With A. Bioy Casares. Buenos Aires: Librería La Ciudad, 1977.
Obras completas en colaboración. Buenos Aires: Emecé, 1979. Not an original work, but a selection of major collaborative works done with Bioy Casares, M. Guerrero, A. Jurado, M. Kodama, and M. E. Vázquez.
Los orilleros. El paraíso de los creyentes. With A. Bioy Casares. Buenos Aires: Losada, 1955.
Seis problemas para don Isidro Parodi. H. Bustos Domecq (pseud. of J. L. Borges and A. Bioy Casares). Buenos Aires: Sur, 1942.

Other Works in Collaboration

Antiguas literaturas germánicas. With Delia Ingenieros. Mexico City and Buenos Aires: Fondo de Cultura Económica, 1951.
Antología clásica de la literatura argentina. With Pedro Henríquez Ureña. Buenos Aires: Kapelusz, 1937.
Antología de la literatura fantástica. With Silvina Ocampo and Adolfo Bioy Casares. Buenos Aires: Sudamericana, 1940. Additional volumes have appeared periodically.
Antología poética argentina. With Silvina Ocampo and Adolfo Bioy Casares. Buenos Aires: Sudamericana, 1941.
Atlas. With María Kodama. Buenos Aires: Sudamericana, 1984.
Introducción a la literatura inglesa. With María Esther Vázquez. Buenos Aires: Columba, 1965.
Introducción a la literatura norteamericana. With Esther Zemborain de Torres. Buenos Aires: Columba, 1967.
Leopoldo Lugones. With Betina Edelberg. Buenos Aires: Troquel, 1955.
Libro del cielo y del infierno. With Adolfo Bioy Casares. Buenos Aires: Sur, 1960.
El libro de los seres imaginarios. With Margarita Guerrero. Buenos Aires: Kier, 1967.
Literaturas germánicas medievales. With María Esther Vázquez. Buenos Aires: Falbo, 1966.
Manual de zoología fantástica. With Margarita Guerrero. Mexico City and Buenos Aires: Fondo de Cultura Económica, 1957.
El "Martín Fierro." With Margarita Guerroro. Buenos Aires: Columba, 1953.
Los mejores cuentos policiales. With Adolfo Bioy Casares. Buenos Aires: Emecé, 1943. Additional volumes have appeared periodically.
The Aleph and Other Stories (1933-1969). Edited and translated by Norman Thomas di Giovanni in collaboration with the author. New York: Dutton, 1970.

Principal Translations in English

Atlas. Translated and annotated by Anthony Kerrigan. New York: Dutton, 1985.

The Book of Sand. Translated by Norman Thomas di Giovanni. New York: Dutton, 1977.

Doctor Brodie's Report. Translated by Norman Thomas di Giovanni in collaboration with the author. New York: Dutton, 1972.

Dreamtigers. Translated by Mildred Boyer and Harold Morland. Austin: University of Texas Press, 1964. The translation of *El hacedor.*

Evaristo Carriego: A Book about Old-Time Buenos Aires. Translated by Norman Thomas di Giovanni with the assistance of Susan Ashe. New York: Dutton, 1983.

Ficciones. Translated by Anthony Kerrigan and others. New York: Grove Press, 1962.

The Gold of the Tigers: Selected Later Poems. Translated by Alastair Reid. New York: Dutton, 1977.

In Praise of Darkness. Translated by Norman Thomas di Giovanni. New York: Dutton, 1974.

Labyrinths: Selected Stories and Other Writings. Edited by Donald A. Yates and James E. Irby. New York: New Directions, 1962.

Other Inquisitions 1937–1952. Translated by Ruth L. C. Simms. Austin: University of Texas Press, 1964.

A Personal Anthology. Edited by Anthony Kerrigan. New York: Grove Press, 1967.

Selected Poems 1923–1967. Translated by Norman Thomas di Giovanni and others. New York: Delacorte Press, 1972.

A Universal History of Infamy. Translated by Norman Thomas di Giovanni. New York: Dutton, 1972.

SECONDARY WORKS

Interviews

Barnstone, Willis. *Borges at Eighty: Conversations.* Bloomington: Indiana University Press, 1982. Twelve interviews by various critics and writers all of recent (1980) vintage.

Burgin, Richard. *Conversations with Jorge Luis Borges.* New York: Holt, Rinehart and Winston, 1969. Widely quoted and translated into Spanish, Italian, and French, this is one of the most important of Borges's interviews.

Charbonnier, Georges. *Entretiens avec Jorge Luis Borges.* Paris: Gallimard, 1967. A Spanish translation of this important series of French radio interviews is available as *El escritor y su obra; entrevistas con Jorge Luis Borges*. Mexico City: Siglo XXI, 1967.

Di Giovanni, Norman Thomas, and others. *Borges on Writing*. New York: Dutton, 1973. Sessions with students enrolled in a graduate writing program at Columbia University.

Sorrentino, Fernando. *Siete conversaciones con Jorge Luis Borges*. Buenos Aires: Casa Pardo, 1973. Intelligently framed questions yield interesting answers in this extensive interview.

Vázquez, María Esther. *Borges: imágenes, memorias, diálogos*. Caracas: Monte Avila, 1977. A group of conversations held at various times with Vázquez, a close friend of the Borges family.

Bibliographies

Barrenechea, Ana María. "Bibliografía" in *La expresión de la irrealidad en la obra de Jorge Luis Borges*. Mexico City: El Colegio de México, 1957. Valuable for dating and locating earlier items published separately in various periodicals and newspapers.

Becco, Horacio Jorge. *Jorge Luis Borges: Bibliografía total*. Buenos Aires: Pardo, 1973. Much of the information is superseded by Foster, but reproductions of title pages and other iconography make this volume valuable.

Foster, David William. *Jorge Luis Borges: An Annotated Primary and Secondary Bibliography*. Introduction by Martin S. Stabb. New York and London: Garland, 1984. The most complete bibliography to date, indispensable for serious students of Borges.

Books and Parts of Books

Alazraki, Jaime. *La prosa narrativa de Jorge Luis Borges*. Madrid: Gredos, 1968. Certainly one of the most basic monographs on the early canonical prose.

Alter, Robert. *Partial Magic: The Novel as a Self-Conscious Genre*. Berkeley, Los Angeles, and London: University of California Press, 1975. An important study of metafiction in which Borges figures prominently.

Balderston, Daniel. *The Literary Universe of Jorge Luis Borges: An Index to References and Allusions to Persons, Titles, and Places in His Writings*. Westport, Conn.: Greenwood Press, 1986. An extremely important vade mecum for students of Borges.

Barrenechea, Ana María. *La expresión de la irrealidad en la obra de Jorge Luis Borges*. Mexico City: El Colegio de México, 1957. One of the first surveys of the main themes in Borges's work, with emphasis on the prose. Excellent bibliography. The English translation by Robert Lima is titled *Borges the Labyrinth Maker*. New York: New York University Press, 1965.

Bell-Villada, Gene. *Borges and His Fiction: A Guide to His Mind and Art*. Chapel Hill: University of North Carolina Press, 1981. A solid comprehensive study that includes considerable material on Borges's life and times and some interesting comment on the later prose.

Christ, Ronald. *The Narrow Act: Borges's Art of Allusion.* New York and London: New York University Press, 1969. An excellent study focusing on allusion and what has come to be called "intertextuality." Widely quoted.

Cohen, J. M. *Borges.* New York: Barnes and Noble, 1974. A rather short but very sensible overview of Borges's work.

Crosson, John Dominic. *Raid on the Articulate: Comic Eschatology in Jesus and Borges.* New York: Harper and Row, 1976. Sophisticated textual analysis based on the notion of a kind of parallelism between the iconoclasm of Jesus and that of Borges.

Donoso, José. *The Boom in Spanish American Literature: A Personal History.* Translated by G. Kolovakos. New York: Columbia University Press, 1977.

Fernández Moreno, César. *Esquema de Borges.* Buenos Aires: Perrot, 1957. Rather short schematic essay on Borges's total production to that date. Neither overly critical nor very laudatory.

Fokkema, Douwe W. *Literary History, Modernism and Postmodernism.* Amsterdam and Philadelphia: J. Benjamins, 1984. A study of the indicated movements, with several important references to Borges.

Foucault, Michel. *Language, Counter-Memory, Practice.* Translated by Donald F. Bouchard and Sherry Simon. Ithaca, N.Y.: Cornell University Press, 1977. English translation of several important essays, with a number of interesting references to Borges.

————. *The Order of Things.* New York: Vintage, 1973. Translation of an important basic work, *Les mots y les choses,* by this influential French thinker. In the preface Foucault clarifies his debt to Borges.

Genette, Gérard. *Figures.* Paris: Ed. du Seuil, 1966. Basic work by the celebrated French theorists. Includes several significant references to his readings of Borges.

Gertel, Zunilda. *Borges y su retorno a la poesía.* Mexico City: De Andrea, 1968. One of the first monographs focused exclusively on Borges as a poet.

Gutiérrez Girardot, Rafael. *Jorge Luis Borges, ensayo de interpretación.* Madrid: Insula, 1959. Interpretative rather than technical. A sympathetic presentation of Borges's sense of irony and caricature.

Jurado, Alicia. *Genio y figura de Jorge Luis Borges.* Buenos Aires: Ed. Universitaria de Buenos Aires, 1964. Anecdotal and informal rather than scholarly, but with valuable insights into the man and his work.

Lindstrom, Naomi. *Jorge Luis Borges: A Study of the Short Fiction.* Boston: Twayne Publishers, 1990. Helpful analysis of virtually all the short fiction, including the less frequently discussed texts.

Molloy, Silvia. *La diffusion de la littérature hispano-américaine en France au XX siècle.* Paris: Presses Universitaires de France, 1972. An excellent general

study of the reception of Spanish American letters in France. The chapter on
Borges (pp. 194–247) is very valuable and well documented.
————. *Las letras de Borges*. Buenos Aires: Sudamericana, 1979. A very percep-
tive analysis of his narrative techniques.
Prieto, Adolfo. *Borges y la nueva generación*. Buenos Aires: Letras Universitarias,
1954. One of the first book-length studies of Borges, and highly critical of
him.
Rodríguez Monegal, Emir. *Jorge Luis Borges: A Literary Biography*. New York:
Dutton, 1978. An indispensable work for relating Borges's life to his texts.
Ríos Patrón, José Luis. *Jorge Luis Borges*. Buenos Aires: La Mandrágora, 1955.
A rather partisan defense of Borges against those who considered him aloof or
"inhuman."
Sucre, Guillermo. *Borges el poeta*. Mexico City: University Nacional Autónoma
de México, 1968. Stresses the relationships between the poetry and the prose
and emphasizes the "intimate" quality of Borges's poetry.
Stabb, Martin S. *Jorge Luis Borges*. New York: Twayne, 1970. The first study in
English to examine Borges's poetry, narratives, and essays.
Sturrock, John. *Paper Tigers: The Ideal Fictions of Jorge Luis Borges*. Oxford:
Clarendon, 1977. A solid study focused on the canonical texts of *Ficciones*
and *El Aleph*. Offers a close textual analysis as well as consideration of broad
questions related to Borges's theory of fiction.
Tamayo, Marcial, and **Adolfo Ruiz-Días.** *Borges, enigma y clave*. Buenos Aires:
Nuestro Tiempo, 1955. An early study emphasizing the prose. In general,
defends Borges against his critics.
Videla, Gloria. *El ultraísmo*. Madrid: Gredos, 1963. A general study of this
movement with some references to Borges's early poetry.
Wheelock, Carter. *The Mythmaker: A Study of Motif and Symbol in the Short Stories of Jorge Luis Borges*. Austin: University of Texas Press, 1969. A widely
cited monograph emphasizing the explanation of Borges's fiction through
myth and symbol.

Articles

Alazraki, Jaime. "Borges and the New Latin American Novel." *TriQuarterly* 25
(1972): 377–98. An important article in which Alazraki establishes specific
linkages between Borges and the new novelists. Reprinted in the collection
Prose for Borges (1974).
Barth, John. "The Literature of Exhaustion." *Atlantic,* August 1967, 29–34. A
very provocative article on Borges and the state of literature in the mid-1960s.
, Very frequently cited.
————. "The Literature of Replenishment: Postmodernism and the Rebirth of
the Novel." *Atlantic* September 1980, 65–71. A companion piece to his earlier "Literature of Exhaustion." Barth points out the "misreadings" of his

1967 essay and suggests that Borges may be the last of the modernists and a bridge between two centuries.

Caws, Peter. "Structuralism." In *Dictionary of the History of Ideas,* edited by P. P. Wiener, vol.4: 322–30. New York: Scribners, 1973. Encyclopedia article defining this movement.

Cela, Camilo José. "Buenos Aires o un mar sin orillas." *Indice,* 30 January 1953, 2. Brief article by the Spanish novelist and Nobel laureate, highly critical of Borges.

Christ, Ronald J. "The Art of Fiction: Jorge Luis Borges." *Paris Review* 40 (1967): 116–64. Actually an interview, but one in which Christ expounds some of his own ideas on Borges's fiction.

—————. "Forking Narratives." In *Simply a Man of Letters,* edited by Carlos Cortínez, 75–88. Orono: University of Maine Press, 1982. In addition to discussing his narrative structure, Chirst takes up the question of Borges's influence on specific North American writers. Appeared originally in *Latin American Literary Review* 14 (1979).

de Man, Paul. "A Modern Master." In *Modern Critical Views: Jorge Luis Borges,* edited by Harold Bloom, 21–27. New York: Chelsea House, 1986. A good example of early critical acclaim for Borges in the United States. Originally published in *New York Review of Books* 19 (1964).

Foster, David W. "Borges and Structuralism: Toward an Implied Poetics." *Modern Fiction Studies* 19 (1973): 341–51. Foster relates Borges's underlying aesthetic and rhetorical principles to the basic ideas of structuralism.

—————. "Toward a Characterization of *Écriture* in the Stories of Borges." In his *Studies in the Contemporary Spanish American Short Story,* 13–30. Columbia: University of Missouri Press, 1979. Suggests how the structuralist concept of *écriture* can be profitably applied to Borgesian texts.

Frank, Roslyn M., and Nancy Vosburg. "Textos y Contra-textos en 'El jardín de senderos que se bifurcan.'" *Revista Iberoamericana* 100–101 (1977): 517–34. A rather complex structuralist analysis of this famous text.

González Echeverría. "Borges and Derrida." In *Modern Critical Views: Jorge Luis Borges,* edited by Harold Bloom, 227–34. New York: Chelsea House, 1986. A provocative essay suggesting, chiefly on the basis of epigraphs, links between Borges's and Derrida's work, especially his *Pharmacie de Platon.* Appeared originally in Spanish in González Echeverría's *Isla a su vuelo fugitiva* (1983).

Hassan, Ihab. "Pluralism in Postmodern Perspective." In *Exploring Postmodernism,* edited by Douwe W. Fokkema, 17–39. Amsterdam and Philadelphia: J. Benjamins, 1987. An overview of postmodernist letters considered as "pluralism" rather than as a specific movement: several important references to Borges.

Irby, James E. "Borges and the Idea of Utopia." In *Modern Critical Views: Jorge Luis Borges,* edited by Harold Bloom, 93–103. New York: Chelsea House,

1986. Good analysis of "Tlön, Uqbar, Orbis Tertius" in relation to other Borgesian texts. Appeared originally in *The Cardinal Points of Borges*. Austin: University of Texas Press, 1971.

Jitrik, Noé. "Estructura y significación en *Ficciones* de Jorge Luis Borges." *Casa de los Américas* 53 (1969):50–62. One of the best examples of structuralist criticism as applied to the canonical texts. Stresses Borges's innovations and the interrelationships among the various stories in *Ficciones*. Reprinted in Fló's *Contra Borges* (q.v.) and elsewhere.

Masarra, Ulla. "Narrative Discourse in Postmodernist Texts." In *Exploring Postmodernism,* edited by Douwe W. Fokkema, 215–31. Relates Borges's notion of narrative ramifications to European postmodernists.

Rimmon-Kenan, Shlomith. "Doubles and Counterparts: 'The Garden of the Forking Paths.' " In *Modern Critical Views: Jorge Luis Borges,* edited by Harold Bloom, 185–92. New York: Chelsea House, 1986. Excellent study of this story, illustrating how contemporary textual criticism can illumine well-known texts. Originally published in *Critical Inquiry* 6 (1980).

Rodríguez Monegal, Emir. "Borges y nouvelle critique." *Revista Iberoamericana* 80 (1972): 367–90. An important study of Borges's impact on the critical positions of such theorists as Blanchot, Genette, and Foucault.

Rudy, Stephen. "The Garden *of* and *in* Borges's 'Garden of the Forking Paths.' " In *The Structural Analysis of Narrative Texts,* edited by Andrej Kodjak and others, 132–44. Columbus, Ohio: Slavica, 1980. An example of structuralist criticsm applied to the well-known Borges story.

Sábato, Ernesto. "Desagravio a Borges." *Sur* 94 (1942): 7–34. A famous and frequently cited example of Sábato's ambiguous attitudes toward his compatriot.

_____. "En torno a Borges." *Casa de las Américas* 17–18 (1963): 7–12. Sharply critical of Borges's prose, which Sábato considers "tortuous and guilt-ridden." Continues to praise his poetry.

Stabb, Martin S. "Argentine Letters and the Peronato: An Overview." *Journal of Inter-American Studies and World Affairs* 3–4 (1971): 434–55. Discusses the general state of Argentine writing during the Peronist period with a number of references to Borges.

Szegedy-Maszák, Mihály. "Teleology in Postmodern Fiction." In *Exploring Postmodernism,* edited by Douwe W. Fokkema, 41–57. Notes Borges's early contribution to the postmodernist notion of circularity in narrative structures.

Updike, John. "Books: The Author as Librarian." *New Yorker,* 30 October 1965, 223–46. An important, frequently cited early example of Borges's recognition in North America.

Wheelock, Carter. "Borges's New Prose." In *Modern Critical Views: Jorge Luis Borges,* edited by Harold Bloom, 105–132. New York: Chelsea House, 1986. One of very few studies focused on Borges's fiction of the 1960s and

1970s. Perceptively contrasts these texts with earlier stories. Originally published in *Prose for Borges*. Evanston, Ill.: Northwestern University Press, 1972.

Collections of Articles in Book Form

Alazraki, Jaime, ed. *Jorge Luis Borges.* Madrid: Taurus, 1976. Collects some of the most important articles on Borges by Spanish American, European, and North American critics.

Bloom, Harold, ed. *Modern Critical Views: Jorge Luis Borges.* New York, New Haven and Philadelphia: Chelsea House, 1986. Excellent collection of older, often-reprinted essays along with several more recent pieces reflecting critical theory of the 1970s and 1980s.

Cortínez, Carlos, ed. *Simply a Man of Letters.* Orono: University of Maine Press, 1982. Includes papers, *hommages,* and the text of three panel discussions held at a symposium at the University of Maine.

Dunham, Lowell, and **Ivan Ivask,** ed. *The Cardinal Points of Borges.* Norman: University of Oklahoma Press, 1971. Reprint of articles originally appearing in a special issue of *Books Abroad* 45 (1971).

Fló, Juan, ed. *Contra Borges.* Buenos Aires: Galerna, 1978. An interesting collection of essays highly critical of Borges.

Prose for Borges. Evanston, Ill.: Northwestern University Press, 1974. Reprints articles originally published in *TriQuarterly* 25 (1972), a special issue dedicated to Borges.

Special Issues of Periodicals

Books Abroad (Norman, Okla.) 45 (1971). Reprinted as *The Cardinal Points of Borges* (q.v.). A variety of articles by major critics of Borges such as Alazraki, Christ, Irby, Rodríguez Monegal, Yates, and others.

L'Herne (Paris) 1964. An important collection of French, Spanish American, Spanish, and other critics. Contributions by Europeans illustrate the early recognition of Borges across the Atlantic.

Modern Fiction Studies (West Lafayette, Ind.) 19 (Autumn 1973).

Revista Iberoamericana (Pittsburgh, Pa.) 100–101 (1977). Notes, essays, and reviews, including substantial pieces by critics such as Alazraki, Molloy, Foster, Borello, Rodríguez Monegal, and others.

Review (New York City) 73 (1973).

TriQuarterly (Evanston, Ill.) 25 (1972). Reprinted as *Prose for Borges* (q.v.). Notes and articles by Christ, Alter, Wheelock, Rodríguez Monegal, and others.

Index

The Author

Currently chair of Latin American Studies at The Pennsylvania State University, Martin S. Stabb for the last twenty years has taught at Penn State, where from 1970 to 1986 he served as head of the Department of Spanish, Italian, and Portuguese. He earned his undergraduate degree at Rutgers University and received his M.A. and Ph.D. from the University of California, Los Angeles. He taught first at Colgate University and then at the University of Missouri. He is the author of a widely read study of the Spanish American essay, *In Quest of Identity* and has also contributed some fifty articles and reviews on specialized subjects to such journals as *Hispania, Revista Iberoamericana,* the *Hispanic Review, Revista de Estudios Hispánicos, Symposium, Chasqui,* and the *Modern Language Journal.* When not engaged in academic pursuits, Professor Stabb enjoys hiking, fly fishing, and travel.

The Editor

David William Foster is Regents' Professor of Spanish and Director of Spanish Graduate Studies at Arizona State University, where he also chairs the Publications Committee of the Center for Latin American Studies. He is known for his extensive contributions in the field of Latin American literary bibliography and reference works. In addition, he has published numerous monographs on Latin American literature, with emphasis on theater and narrative, the most recent of which is *The Argentine Generation of 1880: Ideology and Cultural Texts* (University of Missouri Press, 1990).